Prayer Laps

Cathryn! You
You rock! You
are an encouragement
to me. Enjoy the road!
in Jesus, Jhn

By John Hannig

Prayer Laps

By John Hannig

Physical training is good, spiritual training is better (a paraphrase of 1 Timothy 4:7-8)

ISBN: 978-1539614241

Table of Contents

INTRODUCTION

I am learning that there are so many benefits to getting a good physical workout. Now, to be clear, I'm not talking about speed texting or playing a high-energy video game. I'm talking here about a real, high intensity, physical workout. One in which I work hard and work up a sweat.

I'm talking about a serious and regular exercise regimen. A real workout. One which elevates both my heart rate and my breathing rate into healthy exercise ranges. Like running on a treadmill.... Running on a track.... Pedaling on a bike.... Swimming laps.... Weight lifting.... Doing sit-ups.... Pushups.... Walking briskly.... It's all about taking better care of this body that God has given me.

My body feels really good after completing an intense workout. I am more relaxed. I am able to think more clearly. I feel more positive. I am refreshed. I notice that my mind, my spirit, and my emotions, all get a boost from completing a workout. But there is something about repetitive exercises that works against my desire to stay in shape. The routine of the workout sometimes causes my mind to wander. I become easily distracted. I start thinking about other stuff. I seem to get lost somewhere far away from the treadmill or the swimming pool. In fact, when working out, I have often had difficulty keeping count of the number of reps or the number of laps I've done.

Let me back up a bit. I am a man, just embarking on his second fifty years. Daily I am finding there is so much more to learn, so much more growing to do. Every new day of life is a gift, every moment. I am in good health – thank You, Lord. And I've been blessed in so many ways. And I don't deserve any of it. I love my Lord and Savior Jesus Christ, and I have given my life to Him. God has provided amazingly over the years. He is so good. My desire in life now is to glorify Him with my life in whatever time I have remaining on this planet.

WORKOUT ROUTINE

I love to swim. Now I'd say I've been swimming regularly for the past twenty years. My love for swimming began in my childhood, at the local community pool and on its swim team. Swimming is now part of my workout routine. It's an excellent aerobic exercise. And it's absent the heavy and repetitive joint impact of, say, running.

Before I established a swimming routine, I'd say I'd be able to do maybe five or six laps in the pool. And then I'd have to stop and catch my breath.

Nowadays, I can reel off sixty or eighty laps, without being out of breath. The improvement is the direct result of an ongoing commitment to swim and to exercise.

PRAYER LAPS

Now, here's where the Prayer Laps story begins. Several years ago, I would go to the pool for my swim workout. It would usually be in the middle of the day and before lunchtime. I would hop into the water and just swim. I started off trying to do ten laps, then fifteen, then twenty. In business, and in life, whatever gets measured gets done. Counting laps provides a measure of accomplishment.

So I'd start counting laps, and swimming. I'd enjoy each and every stroke, and the freedom I felt in the pool. But soon, my mind would begin to wander. I would forget what lap I was on. And often my mind would become distracted, maybe thinking about a problem at work. Or maybe pondering a challenge at home, or a situation a friend is facing. And while my body had a good workout, I'd feel like my mind was scattered and disrupted.

After thinking about this recurring frustration, I thought I might get creative. I thought I might try playing number games to help discipline my lap counting and my mind. Now, I've always liked numbers and mathematics. So I tried remembering lap numbers by thinking about prime numbers, and multiples. And about factors, and divisors. Okay, admittedly that may come across as a bit nerdy. But playing number games did engage my mind to some degree. I tried it for a while. But I found that it didn't resolve the frustration with lap counting.

Since I am also a sports fan, I tried another lap counting approach. I tried to associate a lap number with a player who wore that number while playing the sport. I figured that I could think about that player as I swam that lap. By the end of the lap, if the player was still on my mind, I'd know which lap number I was on. And I'd hopefully not lose my place counting laps.

For example, lap number 3 might represent Babe Ruth, and lap number 23 could represent Michael Jordan. So I tried this approach. It seemed to work for a while, in terms of keeping me on count with my laps. But when I thought about it, it seemed pretty shallow to be thinking of some famous player while pounding out the laps. It didn't seem to stretch or grow my mind. Maybe there was a more creative and life-giving way to keep lap count.

TO GOD BE THE GLORY

Sometime later, an idea came to mind, for which I can only credit the Lord. The idea is to connect lap numbers to people or things that I want to or need to be praying for. This way, as I swim a lap, I am meditating on and praying for that person or persons or situation I've chosen for that lap. I pray – which builds me up spiritually – and I don't forget what lap I'm on. And I get a full workout.

Have nothing to do with godless myths and old wives' tales; rather, train yourself to be godly. For physical training is of some value, but godliness has value for all things, holding promise for both the present life and the life to come. (1 Timothy 4:7-8)

Or, a modern-day Scripture paraphrase, courtesy of my good friend, Rick (thanks, Rick!): Physical training is good, spiritual training is better.

THE PURPOSE OF THIS BOOK

This book further examines and develops this idea of combining prayer with a good physical workout. What was my purpose in writing this book? I wrote it to encourage you and to share this Prayer Laps idea among people who pray, or who want to pray, or who want to pray more. I encourage you to adapt this idea if you're able, and to let God lead you. It may become a gift multiplied... This book presents a way of adding focused prayer to your life, while at the same time avoiding workout boredom. If the result is more prayer and more workout, well then, all glory to God.

This book is offered to the glory of God. It has been written in thanksgiving to Him, because He's the One from whom it came. When you think about it, He is the One from whom all good things come.

CHAPTER ONE:
Prayer

Prayer is a great place to start. Praying is what some of us do, and what all of us need to do. For those of us who do pray, though, I think most feel like we don't pray well, nor do we pray enough.

So what is prayer? I've heard many definitions of prayer in my life. Even definitions I had memorized back in my childhood Sunday school days. But the simplest explanation I've heard, and the one I embrace, is that prayer is talking with God. Talking with God. Not talking to God. Talking *with* God. Picture a conversation between two people. There's give and there's take. You talk, and I listen. I talk, and you listen. Prayer is not necessarily audible, on either end. Although for some it can be. Prayer is a time set aside for me to talk with God.

LISTEN & TALK

I really think prayer is more about listening than it is about talking. For us, that is. God already knows our thoughts, our needs, our wants. But He wants us to talk with Him. He wants us to reach out to Him. God is the One with all the love, all the wisdom, all the gifts, all the power. Maybe prayer should simply be us listening to God.

What does Scripture say about prayer? Well, it says Abraham and Jacob, and Moses, and so many others throughout the Bible prayed to God (Genesis 20:17, 32:9, Exodus 8:9). Even the ungodly Pharaoh asked Moses to pray for him during the "Let My People Go" dialogue (Exodus 8:8). So prayer is and was understood as a desired connection with the Divine.

Most notably, Jesus prayed often, as recorded in the Gospels:

> *Very early in the morning, while it was still dark, Jesus got up, left the house and went off to a solitary place, where he prayed. (Mark 1:35)*

> *One of those days Jesus went out to a mountainside to pray, and spent the night praying to God. (Luke 6:12)*

> *Then little children were brought to Jesus for him to place his hands on them and pray for them. (Matthew 19:13)*

When asked, Jesus taught His disciples how to pray in the familiar Lord's Prayer:

One day Jesus was praying in a certain place. When he finished, one of his disciples said to him, "Lord, teach us to pray, just as John taught his disciples." He said to them, "When you pray, say: 'Father, hallowed be your name, your kingdom come. Give us each day our daily bread. Forgive us our sins, for we also forgive everyone who sins against us. And lead us not into temptation.'" (Luke 11:1-4)

Prayer is a very good thing. Prayer is a necessary thing. If Jesus, the Son of God, thought it important to connect with His Father in heaven, who are we to think we can do without it? Prayer is like plugging in to the Almighty power source. When my cell phone is on empty, I plug it into an electrical outlet, and it gets recharged. When my car is out of gas, I stop at a gas station and fill up my tank with gasoline, and I drive off with renewed power. Similarly, when we pray, there's a spiritual recharge or uplift that happens.

GOD'S PLAYBOOK

A quarterback looks to the sidelines to his coach to find out what the next play will be. That's like us looking to God to learn of His next desired "play" in our lives. There's an inherent humility that goes along with praying. We, the created, are looking to the Creator, for guidance with what's ahead. We realize that we are in need, we are out of gas. And we know where to go to get filled, to get restored, to get renewed. Or maybe more appropriately, seeking and listening to every word that our Father has for us.

One more thing about prayer, it's something we can do anywhere. We don't need to stop into a church, or go someplace special to talk with God. He's everywhere, including where we are. No travel required. Simply seek Him, call His name, reach out to Him. There's no need to schedule an appointment, He's awaiting our call.

So prayer is important, and necessary. But sometimes we struggle to make time for prayer. Why is that? Why is it hard to make time for God? What about Jesus? Jesus was busy. He had just three short years to save the world and establish the church. He loved, He healed, He taught, He touched lives. Do we think we are busier than He is, and therefore don't have time to pray? Honestly, I've thought that in the past, or at least I've acted like that.

FOCUS ON GOD

When I search my heart, I come up with only excuses why I don't pray more. Distractions I allow to get in the way. Decisions I make to go after something else instead. Something which may seem more appealing at the time. But something that will never satisfy as He does.

Yes, we can find the time for prayer. And we are blessed when we do. My morning commute to work is about a half hour in length. I used to have the car radio on all the time. Nowadays, the radio is turned off. I enjoy the silence. I can hear God better in silence. I sing a hymn to the Lord as I drive to work. Yes, I sing out loud. And I take in the beauty of His creation as I drive. I reflect on all He has done, all He has made, how He loves us. That simple beginning connects me to Him from the very start of the day. And it also helps me start my day at work in the right frame of mind. This is an example of just one kind of prayer. There are so many ways we can pray.

A very good friend of mine shared with me an analogy involving prayer. The Christian life is like a three-legged stool. One leg of the stool is Prayer. One leg is the Bible. One leg is Christian Friends. When the three legs of the stool are strong, and of equal length, the stool stands firm. The stool will then firmly support my weight.

However, when one leg of the stool is loose, or perhaps shorter than the rest, the stool wobbles and is unstable. Maybe one's prayer life is not what it should be. Or maybe one doesn't have close Christian friends. But a man with a solid three-legged stool will be able to stand firm and grow strong in the Lord.

HONOR GOD THROUGH PRAYER

So I need to pray. I need to pray more. I need to strengthen the Prayer leg of my three-legged stool. But how do I do that? Not a quick, mindless, one-minute good night prayer at day's end. Not a rote or mechanical food blessing at mealtime. I need to create and protect portions of my daily schedule for simply being with God. If He's really that important in my life – and He is – I need to honor Him by giving Him my prime time, and plenty of it.

Granted, we live in a day and age in which the speed of life seems breathtaking, and almost unlivable. He's always available. I'm the one who seems to have trouble making time for prayer. I am the one who has to stop and remember who I am, whose I am, and who He is.

So how do we fit prayer time into our lives? Good question. We make it a priority. If it's really important, we will make it a priority. We will create time, and we will find time to reach out to Him.

Maybe we will get up a few minutes early to spend the wakening moments of this new day with the One who made this new day. Maybe we will preserve the last hour of the day for time with the Lord, for meditation, for prayer, for reading His Word. What a great way to get ready for bed time, with the Lord on your mind.

The opportunities for prayer abound. There's an old saying I heard from my parents many years ago: it takes two to tango. Now, I recall that they actually used this saying most often when I was young and when a sibling and I were fighting. By telling us that it takes two to tango, they were saying that not just one of us was at fault, and therefore in trouble, but we both were. (Amazing what you remember from your childhood...)

It takes two to tango. It's true. Like talking with a friend on the phone – it takes two. Well, we know God is there, always, awaiting our call. He's available and He's ready. Are we?

WHEN WE PRAY

One final thought on prayer, for now. Think about the relationship between my Father in heaven and me, His child, here on earth. I am blessed to be a father of an amazing son, named Andrew. It is so gratifying to me that my son also loves the Lord. My relationship with my son, even with all of my shortcomings and imperfections, brings me a new level of understanding regarding my relationship with my perfect Father in heaven.

So what is God's reaction when we pray? I think it's a lot like my reaction when my son calls me or writes to me. I really love to hear from my son. At the same time, I want to honor his life and his time, and respect his space.

He's now married to a wonderful and godly woman, named Alyssa, and they have settled out of state. But ever since he went away to college, I have tried not to be one of those helicopter parents, always hovering over their kids' shoulders. I know I will always be his dad. And I am confident that, as an adult, he is very capable of doing well and making good decisions on his own.

That said, I try to be always available to him. When he calls, I try to drop what I'm doing and pick up. Regardless of if I'm at work, or something else. It is always so good to hear his voice. It lifts me up when he calls, when he reaches out to me. I am always so thankful when he does. It blesses me.

Prayer time with God is much like that. God does not barge into our lives uninvited and take over control and make decisions for us. Quite the contrary. But how much I think it pleases Him when we reach out to Him. It shows Him we want time with Him. We believe we need Him in our life. We seek His will. We love Him. God blesses our prayer time, our time with Him. And in ways we'll never fully comprehend.

CHAPTER TWO:
Workout

OK, so prayer is an absolutely critical ingredient in our lives, and one often overlooked or underutilized. Next we consider working out, or exercising. Now, I work out at a local gym several days a week. I've often thought about the wide variety of people I see at the gym. I sometimes wonder why they are there. Some, I think, are there so they'll be seen by others. Others are there to gawk at others. Still others are there for an actual workout.

BENEFITS OF EXERCISE

So why do we exercise? Some people exercise to lose weight, or to fit into those jeans or that dress. Some exercise to keep their muscle tone, or to look good. Some exercise to increase their physical ability, for example, in being better able to play a sport, or to do work. Still others exercise to feel good about themselves.

In my experience, I've found that, when I feel

good physically, I feel good in the other areas of my life, such as socially, emotionally, and spiritually. There's just something about pushing yourself physically, getting the heart pumping, doing a good, hard, long workout, that feels so rewarding after you're done.

I'm not a runner, though I have recently run two half-marathons. From those experiences, I can tell you that the feeling when you cross the finish line is simply indescribable. Joy, success, satisfaction, refreshment – plus you don't have to run anymore, you're done...

What does the Bible say about exercise or physical training?

> *Everyone who competes in the games goes into strict training. They do it to get a crown that will not last; but we do it to get a crown that will last forever. (1 Corinthians 9:25)*

> *For physical training is of some value, but godliness has value for all things, holding promise for both the present life and the life to come. (1 Timothy 4:8)*

The Bible compares spiritual training with physical training of our body. It acknowledges that physical training is good for the body. No question there. But then it quickly states that spiritual training is even better. Even better than physical training.

WHOSE BODY

The Bible speaks of our bodies as not belonging to us. In fact, it says our bodies are actually temples of the Holy Spirit. They are places where the Holy Spirit of God resides. That certainly runs countercurrent to modern human wisdom. It seems like most people believe the following: I am the center of the universe, and my body and everything else I own belongs to me.

> *Do you not know that your body is a temple of the Holy Spirit, who is in you, whom you have received from God? You are not your own; you were bought at a price. Therefore honor God with your body. (1 Corinthians 6:19-20)*

Now, if your body did belong to you, yes, you could make a very good case for exercising it to keep it functioning well. If you want your car to last 300,000 miles, you would take good care of it. You would change the oil every 5,000 miles. You would have a mechanic tune it up at regular intervals. You would give it quality gasoline as fuel. You would drive it carefully and within speed limits. Because you know that caring for your car is the best way to enable it to last 300,000 miles.

Similarly, if you wanted to live a long life, you would take proper care of your body. You would exercise it daily. You would feed it the right fuel, the right foods – the correct food groups, the right portion size, the right number of meals per day, etc. And you would have your doctor perform regular checkups to ensure continued health.

But now, consider that your body does not belong to you. Instead, it belongs to the Holy Spirit of God. It's His temple. It's where He hangs out. If you and I really understood the depth and the implications of that Scripture verse, would we be treating our earthly bodies as we are now?

I like to keep a nice, clean, comfortable house. But if I knew God was coming to my house later today, I would stop what I am doing right now and start tidying up my house. I would want for it to be spotless and welcoming when He got there. I would want to offer my very best to Him.

HONOR GOD WITH OUR BODIES

It should be the same way with our own bodies. Or, rather, His body. How would I treat it? How should I treat it? I think I would give it my very best, keep it in top notch condition. Keep it flexible and strong and capable of doing anything He asks me to do with it. Keep it in ready condition to serve Him in whatever way He asks. I would honor Him with the body He has provided for me, and give glory to Him in the way I use it.

Let me offer an extreme contrast, to make a point. We're talking about taking better care of our bodies. What happens if we take lousy care of our bodies? If we don't take care of our bodies at all, it will likely lead to a shortened life, an unhealthy life, a life of limited mobility, a life of limited ability. It would handcuff the Holy Spirit, whose temple it is.

Rather than give glory to God, you would be effectively limiting what He might accomplish through you.

So what does that all mean when I consider what to do today. I have been blessed with a choice about how I use my life today. Am I doing a good job maintaining this body, this temple of the Holy Spirit?

I must admit, there is a part of me that really likes relaxation and comfort. I like to relax, to hang out with friends, to watch college football on TV, to play guitar and sing, to read. As good as some of that is, if I sit around all day, and do just that, I will grow weak, and probably round, too. And the inertia toward complacency will grow.

Life is all about balance. Relaxing or watching football is so much more rewarding after a good physical workout, like raking leaves. I need both relaxing time and exercising time. And I need to feed both the body and the spirit.

In the months before I picked up pen and paper and began to write Prayer Laps, I could tell that I needed to exercise more. I needed to make it a priority. Then I needed to do it, to work hard, get sweaty and begin to push my physical limits. No pain, no gain. I needed to gain. I needed to improve the condition of this temple. And I needed to do it now.

CHAPTER THREE:
Prayer Workout

Whether we know it or not, each of us has a deep need for real prayer. Why don't we pray more? Some would say they cannot make time for it. They feel their lives are too busy, too full to stop and pray. Some might say prayer is boring. Some might say it's a waste of time, or they simply question the benefit of it. Some might offer that they're not good at it, so they shy away from it. When you boil it down, and consider what prayer really is, the excuses for not praying become weak and thin.

At the same time, each of us has a strong need for exercise. If one is unwilling to admit that for himself or herself, a quick look around will convince you otherwise. America today is an overweight and sedentary population. Perhaps that's a consequence of eating more than we should. Maybe no portion control. Perhaps we're eating the wrong kinds of foods. Too many fast food meals. Not enough vegetables and fruits. Perhaps we're exercising less than we should, and maybe not at all.

A friend explained it to me this way. Back in the Cro-Magnon days, man was very active. Man had to be active and mobile, in order to hunt, fish, grow, provide food and water for sustenance, provide shelter, and defend himself. There were no fitness clubs or gyms around in those days. There was no need for any of that.

GET ACTIVE

Fast forward to today. Many of us, by and large, sit at a desk or at a computer screen. We answer and/or make phone calls, or read, or write. We tend to do sedentary things at work and at home. We have a strong need to get outside, to breathe fresh air, to walk, to run, to exercise.

Let's think about exercise a bit. What do you think of when you think of exercising? Are you picturing a fun and fulfilling outing, something you're pumped up to go do, and even more energized when you're done? Do you see the benefits as immediate and obvious?

How do you feel before you exercise? And how do you feel when you're done exercising? I'm going to go out on a limb here and postulate that most people feel good after they've exercised. That's how I feel when I complete a good workout. The blood is flowing, I'm breathing heavy, my body feels like it's been worked over, and my muscles are feeling it. And, maybe most important to some, once their workout is over, it's time for rest and recovery.

If that's true, then most people would see the end of a good workout as a very positive thing. So what gets in the way of working out? I think it's getting started. How do you get motivated to begin exercising? No pearls of wisdom here. I think you just do it. Just like the sneaker commercial, "Just Do It." Anticipate the benefit, and invest the effort. But just maybe there's a way to get you motivated a bit more each time you start exercising, to get you over the hump as it were.

I need prayer. I need exercise. Consider combining prayer and exercise. Both prayer and exercise work best when applied with discipline.

> *Be joyful always; pray continually; give thanks in all circumstances, for this is God's will for you in Christ Jesus. (1 Thessalonians 5:16-18)*

Pray continually. Pray always.

> *Do you not know that in a race all the runners run, but only one gets the prize? Run in such a way as to get the prize. Everyone who competes in the games goes into strict training. They do it to get a crown that will not last; but we do it to get a crown that will last forever. (1 Corinthians 9:24-25)*

Go into strict training. Train to win the prize.

Perhaps there's a mutual and synergistic

discipline, through which your prayer life gets a boost, as your physical health improves. Perhaps the former boredom present in some physical training can be filled with a fresh burst of prayer. Prayer that is alive, fresh, new, maybe even different every day. Prayer that feeds and develops the soul. Just as exercise hones and develops the body.

PRAYER & EXERCISE

I have found a surprising synergy in combining prayer with workout. When I swim laps, I automatically pray. The chapters that follow describe that in greater detail. Prayer feeds exercise; and exercise feeds prayer. I must admit, there are times when I feel so tired, so worn out, so exhausted, that the very last thing I want to do is to complete a workout. It is at times like those that I often feel the separate inner drive that reminds me I really need to pray. It is the need for prayer that drives me to my workout.

Conversely, there are times when I do not want to pray, maybe because I've been dabbling in sin or just have drifted away from the Lord, and prayer is not the first thing that comes to mind. However, sometimes, in those moments, I get the urge to work out, to swim laps. Along with that now comes prayer.

CHAPTER FOUR:
Lap 1

Come jump in the swimming pool with me. I don't know for sure what initiated my love for the water way back when I was a child. Swimming in the local community pool with my family was a regular part of my summers where I grew up. I remember being on the swim team with my brothers and my sister. I was certainly not the fastest swimmer out there. I remember being, let's say, a bit chunky as a child.

Actually, I remember almost drowning during one early swim meet. I was about 8 years old, and I was asked to swim a 25-meter butterfly race. Now, butterfly was not my preferred stroke. And it was a difficult stroke for me. You need rhythm, a strong stroke and a strong kick in order to repeatedly propel your upper body up out of the water for each breath. Therein lies the problem. That day, I just remember kicking and stroking, but not getting far out of the water. And, therefore, breathing in a lot of water. *A lot of water.* Amazing that I didn't drown. It's amazing that I remember it so vividly. I finished, yes... Coughing out a lot of water.

But I guess time heals memories like that, because now I absolutely love swimming. No, I don't swim butterfly anymore. As if I ever really could... When I swim laps, I do freestyle for the first length of the pool and breast stroke for the return length. I change up my strokes to lessen the risk of joint problems from the repetitive kicking motion.

PRAYER LAP

Now let me define what I mean by swimming a lap in the Prayer Laps context. A lap on a running track is one time around the track, ending at the point where you began. Similarly, a swimmer starts at one end of the pool, swims to the opposite end and then returns to where he started. That's one lap for the swimmer.

For me, though, when I swim prayer laps, I measure each of my laps as swimming just one length of the pool. That way, every time I touch the wall of the pool, I change strokes and advance to the next lap number. Each of my laps takes about half a minute to complete. And that length of time seems to fit well with how I pray when I swim. Hopefully that will become a bit clearer as I describe my prayer laps.

My normal swimming workout is three continuous sets of twenty laps each. In the pool where I swim, that equals one mile. And it usually takes thirty to forty minutes to complete my workout.

I feel so good after that workout. Breathing heavy, yes, but feeling so good. Now what turns my swimming workout into prayer laps is the prayer part. So let me tell you a little about that.

Each lap number corresponds to someone – or something – that I pray for, or pray about, or meditate on while I'm swimming that lap. And each lap number has a specific meaning to me. In the following chapters, I'd like to walk you through my thinking, the meaning behind each of my lap numbers, what I pray as I swim, and how that all works. If you were to apply the concept of prayer laps to your workout, you'd likely have a different set of meanings to number your laps, or miles, or whatever measure of progress you use.

So we begin at lap one, during which I swim free style. It's an important lap, because you need to start strong. But if you start too strong, you'll tire out before your workout is done. To me, what I pray on lap one would have to represent someone – or something – extremely important. What is my number one? What should I focus on for lap one? I thought about that, and asked myself the question: who or what is the most important person or thing in my life?

The answer, for me, was simple: my one is God.

In the beginning God created the heavens and the earth. (Genesis 1:1)

I am the Alpha and the Omega, the First and

the Last, the Beginning and the End.
(Revelation 22:13)

In my mind, it is all about God. He was, He is, He will be. He was there – Father, Son and Holy Spirit – in the beginning. He is there now. He will be there at the end. He is the One who made you and me and everything that is, was and will be. He is Alpha and Omega, the beginning and the end.

God said to Moses, "I Am who I Am. This is what you are to say to the Israelites: 'I Am has sent me to you.'" (Exodus 3:14)

His name is so holy, it was not even to be spoken in early Old Testament times. I Am who I Am. God is the great I Am.

So as I swim lap one, I pray to God, I talk with Him. I still myself to listen to Him, to what He has for me this day. This very moment. I meditate on Him, I reflect on His love, His creativity, His created works, His creatures, His nature. I thank Him for the air I breathe, the water I'm swimming in, the earth He made. I thank Him, I praise Him and I worship Him.

I find myself thanking God for the gift of this day, for the gift of this pool. I thank Him for the freedom to be able to swim in it, for the physical ability to swim. I thank God for the lifeguards, and for a beating heart. You see how easy it becomes to pray when you focus and then free yourself to think and meditate and follow where you're led.

I'll often think of Scriptures which describe God's majesty, and speak them to myself. I sometimes try to imagine what heaven is like, how majestic the throne room of God must be. The key is freeing yourself to pray wherever your heart is led. Now keep in mind I'm praying like this as I swim lap one. So if I somehow forget what lap I'm on, I know how I'm praying. I'm praying to and meditating on God – I'm on lap one.

There's one other thing that's important as you swim and pray. Since a key element in prayer laps is focus, don't be distracted by the swimmer in the next lane who is blowing past you like you're standing still. Don't be distracted by loud noises, or by splashes, or by people just walking around the pool. This time is for you. Time for you to get a good workout. Time for you to have some uninterrupted prayer time. And remember that Satan would just love to distract you from this time of prayer.

TOTAL HEART WORKOUT

A good friend shared with me this insight. Doing prayer laps really provides a total heart workout. Your physical heart is pumping hard and methodically, at a high rate, getting a good workout. And your spiritual heart is being uplifted and renewed as it humbles itself and opens itself in prayer to its Creator. A total heart workout. I like that.

CHAPTER FIVE:
Lap 2

Ok, so we just finished lap one, a free style lap. We touch the wall and push off, and we start lap two. Lap two for me is a breast stroke lap. What do I pray about during lap two? What is the significance to me of the number two? I could see how some might guess that, after giving lap one to God, lap two would be for my spouse. I think there's really good rationale for that, if you have a spouse. Or maybe pray for your future spouse.

I think the most important decision one has to make in life is a decision for God. That is, a decision to give one's life to the Lord Jesus Christ. Admitting that I am a sinner, being truly sorry for my sins, and realizing that the price of my sin is death, that I could not possibly pay the price for all my sins, and that Jesus has done that for me, I accept Him as my Lord and Savior. That decision is number one, by far.

I think the second most important decision in life is whether to marry, and if so, whom to marry. I think all other decisions in life pale by comparison – do I go to college, where do I go to college, where do I live, what career will I pursue... So I can see some people choosing their spouse as their prayer focus for lap two.

And that might have been the case for me, too, except that I am a widower. My precious wife, Nancy, died many years ago, and I've been a single parent ever since. That's another story altogether, for perhaps another time.

NANCY

But let me give you an extremely abbreviated version of that story. Admittedly, it's far short of what the story deserves. Nancy was an incredible woman, gifted in so many ways. Born and raised in Georgia, she had gone through some significant struggles in her young life. And then she meets this nerdy guy from New Jersey (that's me), through work friends. And somehow, they fall in love. It brings both of them back to church and growing closer in relationship with the Lord. They marry. They settle. They have a house. They have a dog. They have a son, the apple of their eyes.

And then Nancy is diagnosed with cancer, shortly after giving birth. And their world is turned upside down. Young couple. Young son. And with so much of life ahead to be lived together. What is going on? Friends and family gather around the young couple, helping in every area of need. The Lord, meanwhile, is busy at work in both of us.

Praying. Praying. Praying. Radical hysterectomy. Radiation treatment. Nine months of chemotherapy. And finally, after a thoroughly exhausting battle with cancer, Nancy died.

PAIN OF LOSS

Yes, there was so much sadness with that huge loss. Nancy died when our son Andrew was 18 months old. We had known each other five years. But, one thing I want to make sure I tell you is that the Lord was there with us throughout the battle. And the Lord used our battle with cancer and Nancy's death from it to get my attention and bring me to a place where I gave my life completely to Him. And for that, as surprising as it may sound, I am eternally grateful.

I believe I will see my wife Nancy again in heaven. You see, she, too, had given her life to Jesus. And several years later, our son gave his life to Christ as well. In retrospect, I daresay that if that tragedy had not happened to my family, I really doubt I would have come to Christ.

> *And we know that in all things God works for the good of those who love him, who have been called according to his purpose. (Romans 8:28)*

Sometimes I think God uses tragedies in life to get our attention. To allow us to see what's important. To come to the end of ourselves. To come to a decision to accept Him as Lord.

Ok, so if my spouse is not my lap two prayer focus, who or what is? Well, it's the Lord and me, the two of us. Let me explain. When I was a young boy, I really loved my dad. I loved just being with him. He died young, at age 50. At the time, I was a teenager, just entering high school. Despite the shortness of time, I have so many warm memories of my dad, and of my time with him.

I remember well the times we played together, and the times we watched Star Trek on TV together. I remember his great sense of humor, and his belly laugh. I remember when, late Christmas Eve, he would make a tape recording on one of those old reel-to-reel audio recorders, creating a really funny conversation between him and Santa Claus. Yes, Santa Claus. My dad would crank up the creativity and color, changing his voice to play both parts. On Christmas morning, we kids would eagerly listen to the recording and try to imagine it all.

And I remember well the many times my dad and I held hands. I don't know what it is about holding hands, but when I was younger, I sure liked holding hands with those I love. I can still picture my dad and me walking together, hand in hand, just talking, or maybe not even talking. Just being together. I can still feel the warmth of his large, strong hand, totally enveloping my little hand. I can also still feel his love, his protection and his care for me.

So that is the image I would typically start

with as I swim lap two, my little hand in my dad's warm and big hand. Just the two of us. Then I'd usually broaden that thought to meditate on a picture of me with my little hand in the Lord's warm and big hand. Again, the two of us, walking side by side. How peaceful. How right. How I feel the love of the Lord, His protection, His caring.

ALWAYS THERE

So much more comes out as I meditate and consider that here is the King of heaven, the maker of the universe, and I'm holding hands with Him. He has time for me. He wants to be with me. He is always waiting to hear from me. God is walking with me. He is walking with me wherever I go. Good places or bad, harsh and hard places, or happy and fun places, He is there.

I think about the expanse of life here on earth and I realize that friends will come in and out of your life here. Even family will come in and out of your life. People will be born into your life, and you will see people die during your lifetime. There will be one constant, one thing you can rely on – and that's the Lord.

Jesus Christ is the same yesterday and today and forever. (Hebrews 13:8)

Have you ever thought of your last day on earth? Unless we're here to see Jesus come again, there will be a day when each of us dies. On that day, in the end, you won't necessarily have your spouse, your children, your relatives, your friends. In the end, you will have the Lord, if you've given your life to Him. And that is an amazing thing.

So it is all the more reason to celebrate your relationship with the Lord in the here and now. To honor that relationship with Him now. Not to wait until that final earthly day to introduce yourself to Him. To know that He was with you before you were born. To know that He will be with you beyond this earthly life and into the rest of your eternal life with Him. And the same goes for your family and friends, if they know Him as their Lord and Savior.

Just the two of you... Lap two.

CHAPTER SIX:
Lap 3

Start of lap three. Back to free style for lap three. Think about the number three. What thoughts does that number conjure up for you? For me, if I search for the intersection of prayer and the number three, I come up with the Trinity. God, three in one. The Father, the Son, and the Holy Spirit. Let's go to the Great Commission.

> *Then Jesus came to them and said, "All authority in heaven and on earth has been given to me. Therefore go and make disciples of all nations, baptizing them in the name of the Father and of the Son and of the Holy Spirit, and teaching them to obey everything I have commanded you. And surely I am with you always, to the very end of the age." (Matthew 28:18-20)*

Now I imagine there are other places in the

Bible which speak of the Trinity. But I like this one. Jesus is the speaker, and He is just about to ascend up into heaven after having died on the cross and risen from the dead. He speaks of three "persons" in one God. And He says that we should go make disciples and baptize them in the name of each of the three persons of what we call the Trinity.

Now I don't believe that any of us as humans will ever be able to fully grasp an accurate understanding of how the "three persons in one God" works. Frankly, I think that it's way above us, so far beyond us, and it'll always be that way. Simply because we are human, and God is God.

GOD > ME

Envision an ant at your feet, looking up to you, a man or woman. The ant says: "I know you, I know all about you." No. That wouldn't happen. That couldn't happen. How could an ant understand and know a human? Now multiply and amplify the difference between an ant and a human. How much greater is the difference between any of us and God. There is no way we can fully understand and know Him.

Nevertheless, there are some clues in Scripture. Some clues about each person of the Trinity: God the Father; Jesus, His only Son; and the Holy Spirit. And it's well worth reading.

So on lap three I swim and I meditate on the Trinity. I spend time thinking about each person of the Trinity, and praying to God in my very limited understanding of each person. I think about God the Father. Now I am a father, an earthly father. And I know the innate drive I have to love my family, to serve my family, to sacrifice for my family, whatever it takes. I would give my life for my family. And I realize I'm a human father. If I, this flawed and imperfect human, have these strong fatherly drives, I can only imagine how deep the Father's love is for each of us, His children.

> *"If you then, though you are evil, know how to give good gifts to your children, how much more will your Father in heaven give the Holy Spirit to those who ask him!" (Luke 11:13)*

In this passage, Jesus draws this same distinction between humans as father and God the Father. How much greater is the love of our Heavenly Father for us than even our earthly fathers. How God longs for us to be with Him. How He would sacrifice anything to save us, to have us be with Him forever. How He would even sacrifice His one and only Son, to die for our sins. So that we could be with Him, Father, Son and Spirit.

Prayer and meditation like this freely flows in my heart and mind as I swim lap three. I meditate on the Son of God, Jesus, and all that He has done for us. He died for us, He died for me. I owe Him my life. Literally. The Gospels tell many stories about Jesus. He healed. He taught. He loved. He served. He sacrificed. He wept. He laughed. He is amazing. I meditate on Gospel stories about Jesus.

HOLY SPIRIT

I sometimes feel like I have a little idea of who the Father is, and a little idea of who Jesus, His Son is, mostly from Scripture and life experience. But when it comes to the Holy Spirit, I feel I know Him the least. I mean, there are many Scriptures about the Holy Spirit and His role:

> *Now the earth was formless and empty, darkness was over the surface of the deep, and the Spirit of God was hovering over the waters. (Genesis 1:2)*

There, from the beginning of time.

> *This is how the birth of Jesus the Messiah came about: His mother Mary was pledged to be married to Joseph, but before they came together, she was found to be with child through the Holy Spirit. (Matthew 1:18)*

There, when Mary became pregnant with Jesus.

> *When all the people were being baptized, Jesus was baptized too. And as he was praying, heaven was opened and the Holy Spirit descended on him in bodily form like a dove. And a voice came from heaven: "You are my Son, whom I love; with you I am well*

pleased." (Luke 3:21-22)

There, when John the Baptist baptized Jesus.

"But you will receive power when the Holy Spirit comes on you; and you will be my witnesses in Jerusalem, and in all Judea and Samaria, and to the ends of the earth." (Acts 1:8)

And before He ascended into heaven, Jesus promised His disciples that He would send to them the Holy Spirit.

But just who is the Holy Spirit in my life? Who is He in your life? Is He that still, small voice guiding you? Does He plant that idea in you to go visit someone in need? Does He come along side of someone who is struggling? Thoughts like that often fill my heart and mind when I meditate on the Holy Spirit, and seek to understand Him better, to better tune my ears to His voice and tune my heart to His gentle nudgings.

What I often notice as I meditate on the Holy Spirit is that I am as a child trying to understand, but being so far from grasping who He is. It leads me into a spirit of humility, a natural kind of humility. Where I clearly see my human limits and am humbled. And yet I seek to know Him more, and to make Him more of a factor in my life.

SEEK GOD

Even after fifty years on this planet, I am so far from grasping who God the Father, God the Son, and God the Holy Spirit are. I keep yearning. I keep seeking. And I think that is a good thing. So by the end of lap three, I am in awe of God, and of each person in the Trinity. And I am humbled.

CHAPTER SEVEN:
Lap 4

Start of lap four. Back to breast stroke for this lap. So what would the number four draw your attention to? For me, the number four reminds me that I'm one of four siblings. My mom and dad are both deceased now, but I think they did a great job in raising us. And we certainly tried their patience. Often. And always...

I had mentioned earlier that my dad died young. I think my dad died of either a stroke or a heart attack. And that thought adds extra motivation for me to keep myself physically healthy and strong. When he died at age 50, it left my mom alone to raise four teenagers.

Think about that for a minute. Four teenagers. And a single parent. My mom was amazing. Yes, I have done the single parent thing, too. For one child, starting at age one and a half. Any success in that came only by the grace of God. Including all of the loving Christian friends and family He provided along the way. But, think about that – my mom was a single parent, starting with four teenagers… Amazing…

I work with teenagers now as a volunteer leader in student and youth ministry at my church and I've done that for thirty years and counting. I love teenagers. But I was a teenager once upon a time, too. I remember back then and I know now how difficult the teenager-parent relationship can be. And I know that my siblings and I really tested my mom. But she stood tall. She persevered. By the grace of God, she would say, time and again.

And somehow, I don't know how, my mom managed to raise us on an extremely tight budget, without any of us realizing it. She was a grade school teacher, and an organist and singer at church; a very gifted woman. Somehow, I don't know how, she managed to see each of us through high school, into college and on to adulthood. I wish she were still around so that I could really thank her for all she's done for me, and for us. She was amazing.

PRAY FOR SIBLINGS

So when I swim lap four, I'm thinking about and praying for each of my three siblings: Marian, Mark and Ernie. Nowadays, the four of us each have our own families and we live in different states. So this prayer connection with each of them is very important for me, since I don't see them that often.

Now when I do more than one set of twenty laps – and I usually do – I repeat the lap one through lap twenty sequence for prayer. And usually my

47

prayers are a little different for each set of twenty laps. That's especially the case for lap four.

So the first time I am swimming lap four, I am praying for each of my siblings, one at a time. I think through and pray for their individual life, their relationship with the Lord, their family life, their work life. I pray for a hedge of protection around them and their families.

The most important thing I pray for each of them individually is for their relationship with the Lord. It's my strong desire to share this relationship with each of my siblings, just as Andrew, the apostle, shared with his brother Simon.

> *The first thing Andrew did was to find his brother Simon and tell him, "We have found the Messiah" (that is, the Christ) (John 1:41)*

Now, I don't know where each of my siblings stands with the Lord. I may think I do, but I really don't. That's between the Lord and each of them. So I pray for their relationship with the Lord. That it is strong and growing. That God is showing them, and that they are seeing, new things daily. A faith that is not growing is dying. And I pray that each of them may shine God's glory in some way, and can be a blessing to someone today.

PRAY FOR SPOUSES

So, for the first round of twenty laps, lap four is for Marian, Mark and Ernie. The second time around, that is, after I've just finished the first set of twenty laps and am on the second twenty, and get to lap four... The second time at lap four, I pray for each of their spouses. I think this is really important. I pray for each of them individually. I love each of their spouses. I care for each of them and their lives here on earth and their eternal lives. So my prayer is first for their relationship with God. That comes first. Always.

After that, I pray for each of them as a husband or a wife. And I pray for each of them as a mom or a dad. If they are blessed to be a parent, and they all are, to me, that would be their most important calling, after the Lord and their spouse.

A parent is the most important person in their child's life. Both parents. That is an extremely high calling. A challenging and difficult calling, for sure, but it's a very important calling. And anyone who is or has been a parent knows that the blessings of being a parent are, well, out of this world.

After that, I pray for each of them in their work, and whatever their daily life brings them. Whether their work is primarily with the children, or whether it is in a hospital setting, or a classroom, or a business, there are daily struggles and challenges. The people, the situations, the problems, which undoubtedly come up. And I pray that they can do their job well, and that in doing it they can be a blessing to others.

PRAY FOR MARRIAGES & FAMILIES

The third time I get to lap four (during the third set of twenty laps), I pray for their marriages and their families. A relationship like marriage is something that needs to be worked at continually. Each spouse needs to work hard at continuing to build their marriage. It is not a passive thing.

There needs to be a constant renewal, a freshness, in a marriage, keeping the heart of dating alive. So I pray earnestly for their relationships with their spouses. Marriage is not something to be taken for granted. It is not something that nurtures itself automatically.

There are so many divorces happening these days, my heart is broken for those broken by divorce. Yet, God intended marriage to be life-long.

> *"For this reason a man will leave his father and mother and be united to his wife, and the two will become one flesh.' So they are no longer two, but one. Therefore what God has joined together, let man not separate." (Mark 10:7-9)*

It's 'til death do we part. It doesn't take a PhD to see how the world is pounding marriages, pounding each of us to not be concerned about others. Instead, the world seems to be telling each of us to care only for ourselves, to make ourselves the center of the universe. That's what Satan wants us to do.

But God tells us plainly that He is the center. We work best when we make Him the center of our lives. It's He, not me.

Lastly, I pray for unity of heart for my siblings and their spouses. Husbands and wives are quite different, and yet they are one. I pray that they can be of one mind in making decisions, that they can really enjoy each other as a gift from God, and that they can truly work and serve each other in a loving and sacrificial way.

CHAPTER EIGHT:
Laps 5 & 6

Now I'm going to combine laps five and six for discussion, and I think you'll see why. Well, let me start at lap six. When I was first thinking about lap five and lap six, the number six meant something significant to me. Six was the number my son Andrew wore on his high school ice hockey jersey, and on subsequent ice hockey teams. Now, since I was a single parent of a single child, you'd think I would follow my son and his sporting endeavors very closely. That's certainly true, but that doesn't tell the half of it.

I love my son so much. I've been coach, cheerleader, teacher, encourager, driver, Scout leader and friend. But more than all of that, I've been father. And I am father. I realize that role never ceases, but it changes over time. While I feel that I've got so many flaws, as a man, and as a dad, God must have made up for that because my son Andrew turned out just fine.

So I pray for Andrew during lap six. But

what about lap five, you ask? Well, in God's providence, He introduced my son Andrew to an amazing young woman of God, named Alyssa. Alyssa is incredible. And I love her so much. Alyssa is lap five. I am so glad that these two found each other, and made the decision to marry. It's been a huge blessing for this dad's soul.

ANDREW & ALYSSA

Andrew and Alyssa met in our local church youth ministry. It seemed like they liked each other for a while, but did not act on it until a weeklong high school summer mission trip to North Dakota. Now, during that summer, Alyssa and her family were moving from the east coast, where we lived, to the west coast. Andrew and Alyssa wanted to start a relationship, even if by long distance, while finishing high school and starting into college. And so they did. Later they went to different colleges. Alyssa attended Baylor University, in Texas, while Andrew went to the University of Tennessee.

Sometime during Andrew's first semester at UT, he told me over the phone that he thought God was telling him to transfer to Baylor. Now, any Christian parent wants his son or daughter to develop ears to hear the Lord. But because of what he said the Lord was telling him, I had to think twice. I think any parent would appreciate this part of the story. When Andrew told me that God said Baylor, I listened and tried not to chuckle. Not because I didn't think it was true, but because I had been expecting this, knowing they were really drawn to each other.

So I told Andrew that what he was saying could indeed be true. That voice he heard could indeed be God. But then again, I told him, that voice he heard could be Alyssa. So we needed to be praying about it. I also told him that, if God was indeed calling him to transfer to Baylor, God would align our hearts, minds and spirits on that decision. Those words, I think, were an amazing gift of wisdom, which came from Someone far greater than me. Well, God did precisely that. He aligned our hearts, minds and spirits. And the rest is history.

You may recall from an earlier chapter, I wrote that I believed the two most important decisions a person had to make in this life were: (1) the decision to give their life to Jesus Christ, and (2) the decision to marry or not, and if so, whom to marry. Well, I can tell you that these two have nailed these two most important decisions of life. They've given their lives to Jesus, and they've married each other. I cannot think of anything that would bring joy to a parent quite as much as that has.

> *I have no greater joy than to hear that my children are walking in the truth. (3 John 4)*

CORD OF THREE STRANDS

Just before Andrew and Alyssa got married, I gave them a symbolic present, a short length of rope. The rope was thick, and woven of three strands tightly wrapped together.

> *Also, if two lie down together, they will keep warm. But how can one keep warm alone? Though one may be overpowered, two can defend themselves. A cord of three strands is not quickly broken. (Ecclesiastes 4:11-12)*

The three strands of the rope represent Andrew, Alyssa and the Lord. And the three strands wrapped tightly together stand strong. To me, it's a strong reminder that husband and wife need to be unbreakably bound together with each other and with the Lord.

One more thing. The number five comes before the number six. That order is also important and appropriate, because Andrew seeks to put Alyssa first. And that's how it should be. After the Lord, the husband should always put the wife first.

So what kinds of things do I pray for during laps five and six? Well, one thing I try to do is to give Alyssa her own lap, and to give Andrew his own lap. In other words, I pray for them individually first. I pray for their individual relationship with the Lord, that it would be ever growing. I pray for their day and for their safety. I pray for the challenges they may face today, and for God to provide for them in a daily way. I pray for each of them to seek God, and to grow in Him continually, and to keep Him first in their lives.

I pray for them in their relationships with

each other. I pray for them to have the love and compassion to truly care for each other tirelessly. I pray for them to know how to nurture and grow their relationship with each other. I pray for them to have wisdom, and to be united in decisions. I pray for each of them to really enjoy this great gift of a godly marriage, and to keep this gift ever fresh and new.

I pray for them in their relationships with their friends, their work colleagues, their neighbors, their church. I pray for their protection, physically, emotionally and spiritually. I pray that they may see the Lord's hand clearly today in some new way. I pray that they may be a shining light, a beacon that the Lord would use for His own purposes. I pray for a strong hedge of protection surrounding each of them individually, and together in their marriage.

I thank the Lord for the gift that each one is to the other. I thank the Lord for how He has led them individually and together as one. And I thank the Lord for all He has in store for them.

One more story, to illustrate my love for Alyssa. The word "daughter-in-law" does not do it justice. She's really more like a daughter to me. Once Andrew decided he wanted to ask Alyssa to marry him, he started planning how he was going to do that. He planned to sit with Alyssa's dad and ask him for her hand in marriage. He wanted to do this right.

He thought about the engagement ring he wanted to buy for Alyssa. His college student finances fell short of what he wanted. So he asked me if he could have his mom's wedding ring, and mine, so that he could use the gold towards Alyssa's ring.

Now that might come across as a little cold and unsentimental, but I appreciated his honesty and his creative thinking. I gave him the rings, including an opal engagement ring I had given to his mom. I asked him to return the opal stone to me if he did not need that for purchasing Alyssa's ring. So he bought Alyssa's engagement ring, and he returned his mom's opal stone to me.

In the meantime, I proceeded to arrange for the opal stone to be placed into a setting for a necklace for Alyssa. I asked Alyssa's mom what type of necklace and what length Alyssa would like, and all was readied.

WELCOME GIFT

At the rehearsal dinner the night before their wedding, I planned to give Alyssa the gift of this opal stone necklace. As family and friends watched and listened, I gave Alyssa the necklace and told the story behind it. I told her that even though Andrew's mom could not be here physically, she was here in some sense. And that Nancy would totally love Alyssa and welcome her to our family. And her opal stone is a reminder of that.

Honestly, I'm not sure if I got all of that out in a way which was understandable. And yes, I certainly did get choked up.

CHAPTER NINE:
Lap 7

Seven is my favorite number. When I was a boy playing Little League baseball, I wore the number seven in honor of my favorite baseball player, Mickey Mantle. So you'd expect something good for my lap seven. So true, you'll see. Biblical scholars tell us that the number seven is used symbolically in the Bible to indicate completeness. For example:

> *By the seventh day God had finished the work*
> *he had been doing; so on the seventh day he*
> *rested from all his work. (Genesis 2:2)*

Genesis chapters 1 and 2 tell the story of Creation. Each day, God created something different. And at the end of each day, He said it was good, or it was very good. Then on the seventh day, He finished, and He rested from His work of creation. Completion on the seventh day. Let's fast forward from the Old Testament to the New Testament. To another major completion:

> When he had received the drink, Jesus said,
> "It is finished." With that, he bowed his head
> and gave up his spirit. (John 19:30)

The story here, of course, is Jesus's death on the cross and His resurrection. Jesus is dying on the cross. After being humiliated and tortured, He is put to death on perhaps the most terrible death machine that man has ever invented. It was maximum suffering in a most public venue. The level of physical pain He endured must have been off the charts.

In His death on the cross, Jesus paid the price for my sins, and for yours. He paid the price we could not pay. He died for each of us. Our sins deserved death, our death:

> For the wages of sin is death... (Romans
> 6:23a)

Jesus died our death. Incredible love. Superhuman love. Unfathomable love.

COLOR OF LOVE

I try to explain it this way to my junior high Sunday school students: black, covered by red, covered by white. To illustrate the point, I'll sometimes use a black towel, then cover it with a red towel and then cover it with a white towel.

Black: the color of my soul, filled with sin. If white is purity and perfection, and black is the opposite of that, black is sin. So my soul is black. There's no question about that. When I consider all my sins of the past, my present sins, and my future sins – even though I try not to sin, I know I still will – it magnifies what Jesus did for me. And it magnifies the love of my Savior for me. Black means that I realize that I am a sinner, that my soul is black. If heaven is white (perfection and purity), black does not belong in heaven. And nothing I can do can make my black into white.

Red: the color of blood. The color of the blood of Jesus, poured out for me, and for you. Jesus took my bullet. Jesus died my death. Jesus, sinless perfection, God and man, came down to earth, lived as one of us and died for us. When I admit I am a sinner and claim the Lordship of Jesus over my life, when I claim His death for my sins – past, present and future – His blood literally covers me. Red covers the black.

> *For the wages of sin is death, but the gift of God is eternal life in Christ Jesus our Lord. (Romans 6:23)*

White: the color of perfection, purity, heaven. When I claim Jesus as my Lord and Savior, my sin (black) is covered by Jesus's blood (red). When the Father looks down upon me from heaven, He no longer sees my blackness, my sin. Rather, He sees white. He sees Jesus's perfection, Jesus's purity,

Jesus's sinlessness. He sees white. White covers red covers black. And I now belong in heaven. Thank You, Jesus.

> *But if we walk in the light, as he is in the light, we have fellowship with one another, and the blood of Jesus, his Son, purifies us from all sin. (1 John 1:7)*

So when I swim lap seven, I easily get lost in meditating on Jesus. I think about who He is. Son of God. Messiah. I think about what He has done for us, for each of us. For us, whether or not we accept Him as Lord and Savior. He is Teacher, Healer, Messiah.

THE CROSS

I think about all the earthly trials Jesus went through. Why did He do all that? Out of His incredible love for us. All He endured: all of the painful trials, the terrible treatment, the beatings, the excruciating death on the cross. All that and more. For us.

Despite all of the earthly, physical pain dished out on Jesus, I think there is a type of pain He endured that is far greater than even that. It's the pain of being separated from His Father in heaven.

I try to understand it this way. When Jesus took on all of our sins on the cross, His whiteness became black. His sinless perfection became sin for us. And the blackness of sin doesn't belong anywhere near the whiteness of purity and heaven. So God looked away.

That separation from God, for the very first time ever, since the beginning of time, must have hurt so very much more than anything He endured on earth. The pain of a separated relationship with His Father.

When I really begin to consider all of this, I am almost automatically led into a spirit of worship. My focus is on Him. I praise Him, and thank Him for all He is, and for all He's done. I find myself repeating Scripture verses, worshipping Him. Repeating Christian song lyrics in worship of Him. How can I not worship Him?

RESURRECTION

While meditating on Jesus, I also think about His resurrection. I consider the amazing power with which He broke apart sin and death. Death thought it had Him. But then He exploded out from the grave. An overt, historic, game-changing defeat of death. An explosion of power and victory. Amazing. Breathtaking. Life giving. Thank You, Jesus.

Let me share an illustration from our church high school student ministry. God's given me a love for music and enough gifting and heart to lead worship at our Sunday evening student ministry worship time. Often times, I get a story in my heart or something to share with the students, relating to a message just shared, or to a worship song.

This one evening, I was trying to make the point of how much God loved us to give us His Son Jesus to die for us. God's love is far greater than any of us could possibly have or even imagine. I told the students that God gave us His only Son. I told them that I have one son. And that I love my son. And that I would die for my son, no question.

I told the students that I love each of them. But, to illustrate the limits of my human love, I told them that I would not ask my son to die for them. I would not. I remember this one young girl sitting up front, looking at me with longing eyes, saying to me, yes you would... It nearly brought me to tears... I said no I wouldn't, I couldn't...

How great is God's love for each of us that He did just that. He gave us His only Son, to die for us. Whether we give our lives to Him or not. And Jesus was obedient to the Father. He sacrificed His life for us, sinners. How great is the love that the Father and the Son have for us...

CHAPTER TEN:
Lap 8

So lap seven was all about Jesus, and His love for us. His sacrificial love for us. Jesus lived as one of us, and then He died for all of us. Then He rose from the dead, defeating the power of death once and for all. So, then, it's a free ticket for everybody, right? Well, yes and no. And that's where lap eight comes in.

Yes, I believe Jesus died for each of us, all human beings who have ever lived, all of whom are sinners. He died the death we all deserve. Will all of us then go to heaven? No. The Bible is clear about that, in several places. Here's one.

> *"Enter through the narrow gate. For wide is the gate and broad is the road that leads to destruction, and many enter through it. But small is the gate and narrow the road that leads to life, and only a few find it."* (Matthew 7:13-14)

Jesus is the speaker here. And He was clear in this passage that only few will find the path to heaven, to eternal life in heaven. So what is the distinction? What does it take to get to heaven?

LESSON FROM MEXICO

Let me illustrate with a story. Each summer for the past fifteen or so years, I have joined with others from my church and travelled to Tijuana, Mexico to build houses with Amor Ministries for needy Mexican families. The Mexican families are gracious and welcoming. The work days are usually long and hot. And the work is hard.

When the house is done, our team gathers with the family receiving the house for a house dedication. We pray with the family, as we do each morning before starting work. We thank them for allowing us to be a part of their family for the week. We tell the family the house is not from us. Rather, it is from the Lord.

At the end of the dedication, we give them the keys to their new house. Every family is gracious, yet so eager to accept the keys. And they are so thankful for this free gift. And they need the house desperately. Their prior living conditions had not been good at all. This house represents, in a sense, new life.

I cannot imagine a family not accepting this gift of a new house. A new house is what they clearly need. It will allow, in many cases, the family to stay together. It will allow the family to overcome poverty. It is what they need. And they now receive this free gift. From God.

In a way, the gift of a new house is like the gift of salvation. Jesus died for each of us, to give us salvation, to give us life. It's like the gift of a new house, built just for you. But some of us actually turn down that amazing gift. Can you imagine? The Bible says most turn down that gift. It's like a love letter unopened. Like a personal gift left unaccepted.

FAITH STATEMENT

Let me share a story about accepting the gift of salvation, and a public expression of faith. I had been baptized as an infant. My parents had me baptized at our family church. Now, my parents made that decision for me at the time, the decision to be baptized. As a baby, I knew nothing of what was happening. But if it were up to me now, and if I believed this infant baptism didn't "take", I would choose to be baptized again.

A couple of years ago, one of the amazing high school students in my student ministry small group had come to a decision that he wanted to be baptized, and in a public way. John had considered the available options regarding where and when to be baptized, but none seemed to be what he was looking for.

After considering a number of options, he discovered the answer. He wanted to be baptized in the river that runs behind my house. When I heard his decision, I thought that was perfect. He cleared it with the youth pastor and with his parents, and the plans were laid. It would be a summer time baptism in the river behind my house. We'd have a ceremony, the baptism, and a cookout celebration afterwards. It would be deeply moving and memorable.

So I started devoting time each weekend, getting the baptism area on the riverbank ready. I combed through the area, clearing poison ivy and sticker bushes. I put on a bathing suit and waded into the river to clear out any debris on the bottom of the river, on which people might hurt themselves. I spent many hours getting ready.

While I worked, I thought about John. I was so proud of him for wanting to be baptized, and in a public way. I thought about his family. I thought about the friends and family who would be there. I thought about me. Yes, I had been baptized as an infant. Although being baptized as an infant was my parents' choice, years later I am in full agreement with that decision. I wondered if I should also make some kind of public statement, like being baptized.

I spoke with my youth pastor and with my senior pastor. Both agreed it would be totally appropriate for me to be baptized as an affirmation and acceptance of my parents' decision to have me baptized as an infant. My heart told me it was the right thing to do. I wanted to confirm and declare my love for the Lord in a public way, and this was perfect.

The day came. It was an amazing day. Despite the river being at flood stage, and over the banks, John and another student were baptized, and I affirmed my baptism. Two dozen family and friends looked on. And God was glorified. In my backyard. In the river. Thank You, Jesus. A gift given. A gift accepted.

GIFT OF SALVATION

So, now, back to the pool. As I swim lap eight, I meditate on this precious gift of salvation, offered freely to all. I pray for those who have accepted the gift. And I pray for those who do not yet know Jesus as their Lord and Savior. Unless they come to know Him, they will be among the unfortunate majority forever. Forever. Eternal life, yes, but not in heaven. Quite the contrary… I pray specifically for family and friends who don't yet know Jesus.

By the way, I think Jesus loves each of us so much that He would have died for us even if only one person accepted that gift of salvation. Think about that. He died that all could come to the Father through Him. Yet the Bible says only few will accept that gift. So many Bible stories make the same point: many are invited, yet few accept. Like the parable Jesus tells of the great wedding banquet:

> *"He sent his servants to those who had been invited to the banquet to tell them to come, but they refused to come." (Matthew 22:3)*

> *"Then he said to his servants, 'The wedding banquet is ready, but those I invited did not*

deserve to come.'" (Matthew 22:8)

"For many are invited, but few are chosen."
(Matthew 22:14)

So what happens to those who do not accept
God's free gift of salvation?

"Then the king told the attendants, 'Tie him
hand and foot, and throw him outside, into the
darkness, where there will be weeping and
gnashing of teeth.'" (Matthew 22:13)

It's sobering to realize what awaits the vast
majority, who do not accept God's gift of salvation.
And many of my friends and family may be in that
number. So as I swim lap eight, I also think about and
meditate on what God might be calling me to do. To
help one more person come to know Him. You know,
it's not about finding a treasure or a safe haven, and
then keeping it all to yourself. If you found a place of
ultimate eternal safety and security and love, would
you not want to share it with others and maybe help
guide them there?

I think God puts us in the place we're at for a
reason. He puts us in our family, in our workplace, in
our school, in our neighborhood, for a reason. As my
good friend, Ron, explained it, we are a man or
woman of God, cleverly disguised as a _____. Fill
in the blank for you: you're a man or woman of God,
cleverly disguised as a mom, or a teacher, or an
engineer, or a counselor, or a friend. God has you

there for a reason. And that reason is to glorify Him. And part of that is helping others come to know Him.

And who knows, maybe we're the only one that a friend of ours will listen to, when it comes to God and His plan of salvation. We could be their lifeline, their eternal lifeline. So lap eight is all about salvation. All about redemption. Thanking God for redeeming me. And praying for those who do not yet know Him, that they may be redeemed. Use me, Lord, to help others come to know You...

CHAPTER ELEVEN:
Lap 9

The best description of what I pray on lap nine starts with the following Bible story.

> *Now on his way to Jerusalem, Jesus traveled along the border between Samaria and Galilee. As he was going into a village, ten men who had leprosy met him. They stood at a distance and called out in a loud voice, "Jesus, Master, have pity on us!"*

> *When he saw them, he said, "Go, show yourselves to the priests." And as they went, they were cleansed.*

> *One of them, when he saw he was healed, came back, praising God in a loud voice. He threw himself at Jesus's feet and thanked him – and he was a Samaritan.*

> *Jesus asked, "Were not all ten cleansed? Where are the other nine? Was no one found*

to return and give praise to God except this foreigner?" Then he said to him, "Rise and go; your faith has made you well." (Luke 17:11-19)

There are so many lessons in this story. The story is an amazing story of healing. Jesus has compassion on each of the ten men. He saw their suffering, and he heard their cries for help. And He healed each of them physically.

They were not healed by an instant touch or by a single word, which Jesus could have done. That would have required them to do nothing. They were healed because they followed the instructions Jesus gave them. Perhaps they did so because they believed Him. Perhaps they had nothing to lose.

So all ten men were physically healed. Story over? No, not at all. I think the story then proceeds to its main point. One of the ten – that would be 10% – actually comes back to Jesus to say thank you. Does that percentage amaze you? Why only 10%? Remember now, all ten were physically healed.

Being healed of leprosy was totally life changing for each of these men. In being healed of leprosy, they each went from being an outcast to being back in community. It was not just Jesus giving each of them a gift or a present. When you get a present or when someone does something for you, you've learned the right thing to do is to say thank you. So why only 10%?

This low thank you rate really bothered me for quite a while. And this is Jesus, after all. Now, I try to say thank you to everyone who gives me a gift or does something nice for me. But when I started to think about it more deeply, I realized that maybe I do okay telling people thank you, but how am I doing saying thank You to God?

When I really started meditating on all that God is and all that He has done for me – Father, Son and Holy Spirit – I realize that maybe 10% is a fair number for my response to Him. In other words, how often do I tell God thank You? Well, definitely not even near all He deserves.

LET ME BE THE ONE

So, my prayer when I swim lap nine is basically "let me be the one." In other words, Lord, I'm done being among the nine who take things from You without coming back to say thank You. I need to stop taking things for granted. From now on, I want to be the one. The one who comes back to thank You, Lord, and to honor and worship You.

During lap nine I pray that the Lord would help me do just that, to help me keep coming to Him to thank Him. I pray that I may be given a thankful spirit. That is not a naturally occurring quality in a human being. A thankful spirit is a gift from God.

Now, back to the story. So what happened to the one who comes back to Jesus? First of all, he praises God in a loud voice. He's not shy about it at all. He is not embarrassed. He was healed, he knows it, and he wants everyone to know. He wants everyone to know who is responsible for his healing:

God. Second, he throws himself at Jesus's feet and thanks Him and worships Him. Notice how intertwined a thankful spirit is with worship and praise of God.

In telling this story, Luke does not indicate the nationality of nine of the ten lepers. But Jesus tells us that the one who came back to say thank you, and to praise Him, is a foreigner, understood here to be a Samaritan.

The Samaritans were historically despised by the Jews. So, instead of a Jew, one of God's chosen people, being the one who does the right thing, it's a Samaritan. This detail of the story, a Samaritan being the one who says thank you to Jesus, would not be received well by a Jewish onlooker. It might perhaps even be considered an insult.

But there's more. What does Jesus say after the Samaritan has returned to give thanks? Jesus says: "Rise and go; your faith has made you well." This time, the healing was spiritual. The man's faith prompted him to go show himself to the priests. His faith also prompted him to come back and give thanks to Jesus and worship Him. So the man was healed physically and spiritually. Furthermore, he was a Samaritan, which means anyone at all can do this, anyone can be completely healed.

By the way, a Jewish onlooker's reaction to this pronouncement of wellness by Jesus on the Samaritan for his faith would likely be indignation. Jews had understood that God's salvation was only for God's people, the Jews. But this story illustrates that God's salvation is offered to all. Thank You,

Lord.

So the message of lap nine: let me be the one, Lord. Let me be the one who loves You so much. The one who is so thankful to You. The one who falls to his knees in praise of You. Give me a thankful heart.

NANCY'S BATTLE

The story of Jesus healing the ten lepers brings to mind another healing story. It's the story of Nancy's battle with cancer. We were praying for her complete physical healing from the moment of the initial diagnosis. And, as the battle wore on, our prayers intensified and broadened to include full healing: physical, spiritual, emotional, wherever God would heal.

Throughout our battle, it became apparent that God was using this illness to draw others to Him, through Nancy. He was gracious in letting me see that in a hospital visit from a friend, or in a tough heart-to-heart discussion, or through Nancy's faith amidst the storm. I could see that God was busy at work touching lives: ours, family, friends, and even hospital staff.

In the end, there are those who might simply have said that we lost the battle; that God didn't answer our prayers. But I've come to understand that we won. The physical healing was not granted, but God healed each of us spiritually, and in countless ways that surpassed our understanding. When we pray, we might not always get what we want. But God gives us what we need. God gives us His best.

Thank You, Lord. For this and more. Please give me a grateful heart, and a thankful spirit. Amen.

CHAPTER TWELVE:
Lap 10

On to lap ten. Now there are a couple of things which come to mind for me when I think of the number ten. One is that the number ten is often used as a measure of perfection. For example, an Olympic athlete's performance in a gymnastic event would typically be graded by the judges on a scale from zero to ten. A ten would be interpreted as a perfect routine.

How about the number ten in the Bible? Well, from the story in the last chapter, Jesus heals ten lepers. In the Old Testament, God gave Moses and the Hebrew people the Ten Commandments:

> *Then the Lord said to Moses, "Write down these words, for in accordance with these words I have made a covenant with you and with Israel." Moses was there with the Lord forty days and forty nights without eating bread or drinking water. And he wrote on the tablets the words of the covenant – the Ten*

Commandments. (Exodus 34:27-28)

The Ten Commandments were given to God's people, to establish God's covenant with His people, Israel. A covenant is an agreement between two parties. God would love and provide for and bless His people. And God's people would obey the Ten Commandments, and as part of that they would worship Him and Him alone. Obedience was a key to God's presence among His people. This covenant would later be replaced with the new covenant, established in Jesus Christ. True perfection.

So, on lap ten I sometimes meditate on the Ten Commandments, how God provided for His people back then, and how He provides for us now. I pray that God would give me a strong desire to obey Him. Obedience to God is not a popular thing these days. Never was. But it's the right thing, the God-honoring thing.

OBEDIENCE

A friend once shared with me this prayer: "Lord, make me want to obey You." Obedience to God should not be drudgery. It should not be a "have to" thing. It should be a "want to" thing. But wanting to obey is not a naturally occurring thing. And so I pray for a spirit so in love with God that it wants to obey Him.

This is how we know that we love the children of God: by loving God and carrying out his

> commands. *This is love for God: to obey his*
> *commands. And his commands are not*
> *burdensome, (1 John 5:2-3)*

I think it is through obedience to God that we come to true worship. So I meditate on His Law. I meditate on Jesus and His teachings. I pray about learning how to glorify God with my life.

What else do I pray on lap ten? When I think about the number ten as a measure of perfection, I think about what God's "ten" might be for me in this life. Now, don't get me wrong, it's not like God has not yet given me my "ten." I am not pacing the floor waiting for God to bless me with my "ten." I consider myself incredibly blessed already. So far beyond what I deserve (I deserve nothing). Salvation, life, my wife Nancy, my son Andrew, my family, my friends, a job, a calling, music... God has been so good to me. I am eternally grateful to Him.

But for example, being a widower with awesome friends, I have many well-meaning friends who have shared with me their view of what my "ten" should be. Generally, many of them think that it would be nice if I met a nice Christian woman. And they usually have someone in mind, as they readily share. Their "ten" for me is that we'd meet, fall in love, get married, and live happily ever after. I love my friends...

And honestly, I've thought about that possibility. I know a couple of widow(er) friends who were so eager to get married again that they did that too quickly, and with the wrong person. In so doing, they blew right through God's stop signs, and ended up hurt, divorced or broken.

I view it like this. God's got a great plan for me. It's my ten. I actually think I'm living it right now. I've got a good day job, which I enjoy and I think am gifted at, and which pays the bills. But my higher calling is to work with teenagers: junior high and senior high students. I do that in a church student ministry setting, and I absolutely love it.

It feeds me richly to pull alongside of these awesome students and share what I can about God, about life, about living a godly life. At the same time, of course, I am so richly blessed by these students in so many ways. And they teach me so much. This is my ten.

TOTAL TRUST

To those who would have me marry again, I say this. I think I tend more towards the practical end of the scale. I'm an engineer, so I guess that makes sense. To me, the most likely thing I see happening is that I'll continue doing what I am doing now; and growing along the way. I'm in my second fifty years, and it's fair to say that I'm somewhat set in my ways. I trust I do what I do well, but I pray I can be open to whatever the Lord has ahead for me.

Yes, there's a chance God would lead me to one with whom I should fall in love and marry. And I need to keep that possibility open, while at the same time making no assumptions. What I do count on is this: if God does have someone for me, He will get my attention. I pray He makes it abundantly clear. When He does, I will see what He's doing and follow where He leads. I know I can count on my God, for that and for so much more.

So I thank God for the ten He's given me, this gift of life, and the many other gifts He's given me. I also pray that He may continue to refine me, as precious metal through the fire; that the impurities burn away.

> *"This third I will bring into the fire; I will refine them like silver and test them like gold. They will call on my name and I will answer them; I will say, 'They are My people,' and they will say, 'The Lord is our God.'"* *(Zechariah 13:9)*

I pray that He refines me, so that what is left will be more perfect in its ability to glorify Him. I've got so far to go. I pray that He continues to guide me through whatever the next phase of life is, or whatever He has for me around the next bend. I pray that I might see His hand as He leads.

One final thought. Maybe there's a part of you that can identify with this. I am one who really wants to know what's ahead. Maybe it's the Eagle Scout in me, desperately wanting to Be Prepared, for whatever lies ahead. I want to know what will happen later today and tomorrow. I want to know what God has ahead for me, even months and years from now.

But God's Word teaches me to focus on

today. Today. To count on Him to guide my very next step.

> *Your word is a lamp to my feet and a light for my path. (Psalm 119:105)*

God's Word to me, God's direction in my life comes when I need it. One day at a time. Today. Not a year from now. His Word is a lamp for my feet. Picture a candle lighting the path before your next step. It's not at all like God is providing high beams for you to see way ahead, and around the next bend in the road. A lamp for my feet. And that is entirely sufficient.

God wants each of us to rely fully on Him. To trust that He loves us so much that He will provide exactly what we need when we need it. To experience contentment in Him.

> *But godliness with contentment is great gain. For we brought nothing into the world, and we can take nothing out of it. (1 Timothy 6:6-7)*

I need to rest on His Word, to be totally content in Him. I know He has the future covered. He knows what's best for me. Thank You, Lord. You are my ten.

CHAPTER THIRTEEN:
Prayer Lapse

...pray continuously; (1 Thessalonians 5:17)

You know, it's funny. Well, it's funny to me. A while ago, I mentioned the concept of this book to a close friend. He really embraced it and he encouraged me to go forward and write. I felt good about that. But do you know the real reason for his enthusiastic response? He thought I had said "prayer lapse", instead of "prayer laps". Hmmmm…..

Yes, at times our lives, including mine, often display a lapse in prayer, or even a complete absence. Why is that? Have you ever wondered about that? Why is there this seemingly common drift away from prayer? I think there are many reasons we could come up with. One core reason I've thought about lately follows from this Scripture passage:

> *For our struggle is not against flesh and blood, but against the rulers, against the*

authorities, against the powers of this dark world and against the spiritual forces of evil in the heavenly realms. (Ephesians 6:12)

Prayer is not an earthly tool. It is not like a saw, or a hammer, or a wheelbarrow. It was not created by man. It is a spiritual tool. Its habitat is in the spiritual realm. Yes, it's certainly true that prayer changes things in *both* the spiritual realm and the earthly realm. But it is a spiritual tool, a weapon of spiritual power. It is a gathering and communing with our Lord. In prayer we are coming to His feet, and worshipping, listening, being.

So who is the weapon of prayer aimed at? Who suffers when we avail ourselves of this free gift of prayer, this direct connection with the Almighty? It's a weapon against Satan. As we approach the throne of heaven to spend time in prayer with the Lord, we draw closer to Him, and further from Satan and his wiles.

SATAN'S DESIRE

Satan is and has been and, I think, always will be trying to get us away from the Lord. He will try everything and anything to distract us from the Lord. He will try to convince us that prayer time is without effect. He will tell us that nothing happens when we pray, so why bother. He will try to convince us that we do not have enough hours in the day to spend time with the Lord, or that we have other more important things we need to do.

Satan does not want us to pray. Think about it. Just knowing that Satan does not want us to pray – is that not reason enough for each of us to pray all the more? Yes, indeed, Satan would love for each of us to be in a state of "prayer lapse". That would please him.

Let's look at the Bible verse above in its context:

> *Finally, be strong in the Lord and in his mighty power. Put on the full armor of God so that you can take your stand against the devil's schemes. For our struggle is not against flesh and blood, but against the rulers, against the authorities, against the powers of this dark world and against the spiritual forces of evil in the heavenly realms. Therefore put on the full armor of God, so that when the day of evil comes, you may be able to stand your ground, and after you have done everything, to stand. Stand firm then, with the belt of truth buckled around your waist, with the breastplate of righteousness in place, and with your feet fitted with the readiness that comes from the gospel of peace. In addition to all this, take up the shield of faith, with which you can extinguish all the flaming arrows of the evil one. Take the helmet of salvation and the sword of the Spirit, which is the word of God. (Ephesians 6:10-17)*

The writer of Ephesians, the apostle Paul, makes it clear that this is a battle. We're at war. Not an earthly struggle, but a spiritual war. And the wages of this war are huge.

We have been equipped with armor and weaponry for this spiritual war: the belt of truth, the breastplate of righteousness, the gospel of peace, the shield of faith, and the sword of the Spirit. And we have one more weapon, as Paul continues:

> *And pray in the Spirit on all occasions with all kinds of prayers and requests. With this in mind, be alert and always keep on praying for all the saints. Pray also for me, that whenever I open my mouth, words may be given me so that I will fearlessly make known the mystery of the gospel, for which I am an ambassador in chains. Pray that I may declare it fearlessly, as I should. (Ephesians 6:18-20)*

MEN IN BLACK

We have prayer. Do you recall the movie, Men in Black? It's a funny movie about a CIA-type organization with secret agents who seek out and control aliens living on earth without people even knowing either one exists. In the movie, there's an invasion by a bad alien, who must be fought.

The two agents, a seasoned veteran and a rookie, go to a weapons panel to choose weapons with which to fight the bad alien. The veteran grabs for himself a big powerful looking gun, and then gives the rookie a tiny water-pistol-like gun. The rookie is annoyed and complains about the puny weapon he's been given. The veteran warns him to be careful with it, and tells him that it's very powerful. But the rookie accidentally fires off a shot, which is so powerful that it blows away a part of the building.

POWER OF PRAYER

Prayer is like that. Prayer is powerful. You and I need to avail ourselves of the free gift of prayer more than we're doing right now. We should seek to avoid a "prayer lapse". A prayer lapse occurs when we choose to live apart from prayer.

One more thought on avoiding "prayer lapse." Praying alone is a very good thing. Praying with other Christians is also a very good thing.

> *They all joined together constantly in prayer, along with the women and Mary the mother of Jesus, and with his brothers. (Acts 1:14)*

I am part of a small men's group, which meets weekly for prayer, sharing, accountability and Scripture study. We meet every Saturday at 6:30 AM at a local Starbucks. 6:30 AM, so that we can give God the first part of the day and be back home by 8 AM when our families awaken. Meeting at Starbucks serves as part motivator and part reward for our efforts to rise and shine so early on a Saturday.

Our group gatherings have been consistently

uplifting, a blessing to me in many ways. And our prayer times have been focused and rich. What a gift it is to be able to pray in concert with godly men. We are praying to the God of the universe, who is so eager to just be with each of us. Thank You, Lord, for the gift of prayer.

CHAPTER FOURTEEN:
Laps 11 & 12

We're halfway through a set of twenty laps. On to lap eleven. When I think about the number eleven, nothing really new jumps out. At least nothing immediately. Then I notice that the number eleven ends in a one, just like lap one did. So when I get to lap eleven, I focus my attention on God once again, as I did in lap one.

God: Father, Son, and Holy Spirit. If you think about it, God should get more of my attention when praying than anyone else. So giving Him two laps out of twenty is better than one. Then again it's hardly enough.

It makes me think about the tithe, among other things. The Scriptural tithe is the principle of giving one tenth of what we have to God.

> "'A tithe of everything from the land, whether grain from the soil or fruit from the trees,

belongs to the Lord; it is holy to the Lord. If a man redeems any of his tithe, he must add a fifth of the value to it. The entire tithe of the herd and flock – every tenth animal that passes under the shepherd's rod – will be holy to the Lord." (Leviticus 27:30-32)

The Bible repeatedly speaks of giving generously to God. And yet there's this mention of a tithe, 10%, as due the Lord. There's a fair amount of disagreement these days on tithing. For example, whether the 10% applies to net (how much did I gain this year), or to gross (how much do I have total), and whether 10% is a goal or a minimum. Big difference. I prefer to think of the goal instead as simply trying to "outgive" God. Impossible. But we should be striving to do that. He's given us our lives and all we have, how can we be stingy with Him?

So part of my meditation and prayer for lap eleven is on God, and part is on how I am doing giving back to God. Am I giving energy and time and attention to God? Am I loving and serving His people? What new thing does He want me to do? Am I seeking to see things more and more through His eyes? To what or to whom is He directing me?

The majority of the time, though, lap eleven is focused on God. Worshipping Him. Praising Him. Thanking Him, for who He is, and for all He has done and is doing. Thanking Him for what He has done in my life, and for what He is actively doing today. Realizing how great God is, and yet so thankful that He allows us to approach the throne room and climb up into His lap and call Him Daddy. He is amazing. Lap eleven.

THE TWELVE

Then onto lap twelve. Now the number twelve has several meanings and references in the Bible. In the Old Testament, perhaps the most common reference would be the twelve tribes of Israel.

> *All these are the twelve tribes of Israel, and this is what their father said to them when he blessed them, giving each the blessing appropriate to him. (Genesis 49:28)*

In the New Testament, the most common reference to twelve would be Jesus's twelve apostles.

> *One of those days Jesus went out to a mountainside to pray, and spent the night praying to God. When morning came, he called his disciples to him and chose twelve of them, whom he also designated apostles: (Luke 6:12-13)*

When I swim lap twelve, my first thought is Jesus's twelve apostles. I think about the fellowship Jesus worked to build, and how most of the apostles grew in Jesus's love and went on to do tremendous things for the Kingdom of God in their lifetimes. I think about applications to me. Today.

SMALL GROUP

I serve as a small group leader in my church's high school student ministry. Over the years I have led several groups of young men, with each group typically starting as freshmen high school students and finishing four years later as seniors. Each of these young men of God has been a huge blessing to me. They have helped me to grow in Christ in so many ways. They've helped me even more than I might have helped them, I am quite sure. I have witnessed that there is great power in small groups.

I also work with our church's junior high school ministry. Junior high ministry is a whole lot different than high school ministry. Crazy different. But I love them both. One blessing the Lord continues to show me as these students go from junior high to senior high, is some amazing spiritual growth along the way. It is a real gift for me to be able to see that.

Jesus was the leader of His small group of disciples. In a similar way, I am the leader of my small group of high school students. Before I go on, just to be clear, I don't mean in any way to equate myself with Jesus. He is Jesus, Lord, Savior – I am, well, me. But Jesus tells us to do as He did.

> *Then Jesus came to them and said, "All authority in heaven and on earth has been given to me. Therefore go and make disciples of all nations, baptizing them in the name of*

the Father, and of the Son and of the Holy Spirit, and teaching them to obey everything I have commanded you. And surely I am with you always, to the very end of the age." (Matthew 28:18-20)

And just as Jesus prayed for His disciples, I pray for the guys in my small group.

"My prayer is not that you take them out of the world but that you protect them from the evil one. They are not of the world, even as I am not of it. Sanctify them by the truth; your word is truth." (John 17:15-17)

So when I swim lap twelve, I am immediately transported in thought and prayer to the young men who make up my current small group. I meditate on each one of them and pray for them, in their growing relationship with the Lord. I pray for them to make the decision to accept Jesus as Lord and Savior, if they haven't already.

I pray for them within their family dynamics, with whatever needs or issues there may be in those families. I pray for them in their high schools, where it is often very difficult to live as a Christian teenager. I pray for a hedge of protection around them as the world, as Satan, takes shots at them unceasingly, and from every direction. I pray for them to get into God's Word, and hunger for it, and meditate on it, and grow in it. I pray for them to develop and nurture growing friendships with other Christian men.

I mentioned I've had a number of small groups of high school students over the years. For the first set of twenty laps, when I get to lap twelve, I pray for the guys in my current small group. Right now, they are sophomores in high school. For the second set of twenty laps, when I get to lap twelve, I pray for the guys in my last small group, who are now students in college. For the next set of twenty laps, when I get to lap twelve, I pray for the guys in my small groups prior to that one, most of whom are now in the working world. And on it goes.

I find lap twelve to be a lap rich in prayer, because I'm praying for guys I love and have known closely and grown with. In listening to them I get a good sense of what they're facing. High school students need prayer. I'm also filled with thanksgiving to the Lord for how He's already grown these awesome young men in Him. And I'm filled with hope for all that God has planned for each of them.

Beyond that, I realize that, however much I love these guys, these men of God, I know that God loves them each so much more than I can ever know. He is their heavenly Father. That is so comforting.

JAM SESSION

A final thought on lap twelve. I lead another high school small group, which developed just recently. This small group is the high school ministry worship band. I've been leading high school worship for the past five or ten years. But in the past few years, I've been more focused on encouraging students with a musical gift to step up and share their gifts.

Every month or so, I invite the band over to my house: voices, acoustic guitars, ukuleles. I order a few pizzas and we jam. These high school jam sessions are so much fun. The jam sessions are part guitar lesson – e.g., how to strum a song or finger a chord – and part worship. I give each student his or her own worship song binder, and we all play and sing together in worship of the God who made worship. I have witnessed how God is multiplying that gift in the lives of high school students. God is so good.

CHAPTER FIFTEEN:
Laps 13 & 14

When I think about the number thirteen, my heartbeat picks up a bit. Age thirteen means teenagers. Working closely with teens for thirty years will do that. I love these adults in training. I remember my early teenage years, feeling unsure of myself and insecure. It seemed like everything, especially my voice and my body, was changing, all at once. It wasn't until much later in life that I realized it was all for the good.

During lap thirteen, I pray for my niece Mary and my nephew Peter. Both are high school seniors now. But when I started this prayer laps practice, they were in junior high school. That's why lap thirteen became theirs.

I truly love these two teenagers. They live in different states from each other and from me. So I don't get to see them all that often. It is all the more reason for me to have solid prayer time for them.

Specifically, I pray for each of them in their

relationship with the Lord. I think about their family life, and I pray about that as well. It is difficult being a teenager in today's world. It is extremely difficult to be a Christian teenager in today's world.

TEEN CHALLENGES

Because a teenager is changing in so many ways, and so quickly, it often leads to friction with their parents. So I pray for their relationships with their parents. I pray that love prevails and that openness and honesty flourish. The majority of the influences served up by the world seek to tear down a student more than build him or her up. The home needs to be a place where love abounds.

I think about their lives at school. There are so many challenges being faced by students today: academic challenges, social challenges, interpersonal challenges, time management challenges. It is so important, therefore, that students be grounded in the Lord, be supported by love from home, and have the daily reinforcement of close Christian friends.

While my prayers for their current circumstances continue, I also pray for their future. I pray for a future spouse, if that's God's plan for them. I pray that they keep themselves pure for that spouse, and that their spouses keep themselves pure for them. With all of the worldly sexual pressures pounding an "anything goes" message into their brains, it is critically important that their hearts remain pure and godly.

Therefore, I urge you, brothers, in view of God's mercy, to offer your bodies as living sacrifices, holy and pleasing to God – this is your spiritual act of worship. Do not conform any longer to the pattern of this world, but be transformed by the renewing of your mind. Then you will be able to test and approve what God's will is – his good, pleasing and perfect will. (Romans 12:1-2)

Then, on to lap fourteen. Now to me, fourteen is quite similar to thirteen. But this time I'm thinking junior high students, who are typically between twelve and fourteen years old. I think about my junior high Sunday school class. I love these students.

People sometimes wonder why, after all these years, I still enjoy teaching and working with junior high students. Well, I'm not entirely sure. But I know there's something very special about their immediate and forthright reactions and opinions. There's nothing processed or phony about it.

There's a unique purity to junior high students. I think that, later in their high school years, they will have learned to first process what they're thinking, at least a little bit, before they come right out and say it. So hearing them now is refreshing. Of course, what comes out of their mouths might not be what you expect, or what you want. But it is honest and fresh.

JUNIOR HIGH STUDENTS

So here's what I pray about on lap fourteen. The first set of twenty laps, when I get to lap fourteen, I pray for the upcoming Sunday school class. I envision each of the students and I pray that some part of the Gospel message will get through to them and take root. I'm not always sure what the lesson will be when I swim, but I know God will provide it. And sometimes He does this as I swim.

On the second set of twenty laps, when I get to lap fourteen, I pray for each student and his or her family. Again, I realize that families are all too often under assault from the world. Many families have been broken by death, or divorce, or absence. Many families are single parent families. Sometimes the father is absent physically, emotionally or spiritually. In all that, I pray that a spirit of love prevails, and that the truth of the Gospel is present.

I sometimes hear a student complain about their mom or dad. It's quite normal that there be some friction between teenager and parent. I think that's part of the greater process of growing up. The process of a student growing up to eventually be on his or her own. And the process of a parent letting go.

To help them understand that and their parents, I share with them a story about a baby bird. If you were to hold a baby bird in your hands, you'd want to keep this tiny, defenseless bird warm and safe. So your warm hands would completely enclose the bird, except for its head. But the baby bird grows. And there comes a time later in the bird's life when it will fly and be on its own. So eventually your hands will need to be wide open.

Parenting is like that. For a parent to change from totally enclosed hands to palms wide open is a very difficult thing. It was really difficult for me, as a single parent. And this opening of the hands, this letting go, comes about in a series of small steps, opening the hands inch by inch. Painful both for parent and for the teenager, who is typically dying to get out and spread their wings. But it's an extremely important process. So I pray for students and their parents.

On the third set of twenty laps, when I get to lap fourteen, I think about each student in their school setting. I pray that their schools provide a safe and positive environment. I pray that each student finds good solid Christian friends to surround themselves with, and other caring friends as well. It's so vitally important for our teens and preteens to be surrounded by positive influences.

PRAY FOR PROTECTION

I pray for a hedge of protection around each student in all of these arenas of life.

> *But let all who take refuge in you be glad; let them ever sing for joy. Spread your protection over them, that those who love your name may rejoice in you. (Psalm 5:11)*

With ever-increasing problems, such as

bullying, self-image and issues of sexuality, ungodly media messages and substance abuse addictions, teenagers really need our love and our prayers. But above all else, teenagers need Jesus.

CHAPTER SIXTEEN:
Laps 15 & 16

On to lap fifteen. This lap also brings good things to mind. Age fifteen to me means high school students. During lap fifteen, I pray for two of my nieces, Megan and Erin. Nowadays, both girls are in college. But when I started swimming prayer laps, they were in high school. That's why lap fifteen belongs to them. I love my nieces, and I pray for many of the same kinds of things for them as I did for Mary and Peter on lap thirteen.

Of course, my prayers for Megan and Erin are separate and focused on them individually, beginning with their relationship with the Lord. I meditate on each of them separately, and sometimes get a feeling in my heart about how I should be praying for them. Other times, it's more general.

I pray for their school work, their jobs, safe travel, things like that. As they've gotten older, into college and choosing a course of study, I've been more mindful of praying about what's ahead for them.

I pray that they discover their God-given gifts, and then develop those gifts and use them for God.

GIFTS & CALLING

Several years ago, when my son Andrew was transferring from the University of Tennessee to Baylor University, I learned a lesson about our calling which I should have already known. We were in a large auditorium, with maybe a hundred other incoming students and parents. It was an orientation session and we were all listening to the Baylor president speak about the goal of a student's time at Baylor, and what Baylor will help them achieve.

Having already visited five or six other colleges with Andrew, I figured I knew exactly what he would say. The message I would be hearing would be the same as at every other college we visited: work hard on your studies, so that you can get a good job, so that you can make enough money to earn a living and support your family.

Now that's not an entirely bad message, generally speaking. But when I heard what the Baylor president said, it was much more meaningful than that. Because what he said was amazing, and simple, and yet made total sense.

He said that Baylor will help each student discover the gifts God has given them. Baylor will help students develop those gifts. And Baylor will encourage these students to use those gifts as God directs them. Think about that. Isn't that amazing? And yet so simple. Isn't that what it boils down to for each of us? Even for me, now, at my later stage of life.

God gives each one of us unique gifts. We don't deserve any of them. He gives them to us. Now I don't think God would give us a gift if His desire, His vision was that we do nothing with it. That wouldn't make sense. A gift should not be ignored or wasted.

I believe God gives us His gifts expecting us to discover, develop and use them. And then, to ultimately help in building His Kingdom. Now I've been on this planet fifty years, why didn't I see that sooner? Then again, it's better late than never.

All that to say that I pray for Megan and Erin, and others whom I love, that they each see their gifting and their calling through God's eyes. And I pray that they are wise and that they head in that direction with their lives. I also pray for their future spouses, if that is God's plan for them.

HIGH SCHOOL STUDENTS

Then, on to lap sixteen. To me, lap sixteen is similar in meaning to lap fourteen. In lap fourteen, I was praying for the students in my junior high Sunday school class. In lap sixteen, I am praying for the high school students I work with in our church student ministry. Again, high school is a very difficult place to live and grow as a Christian. All the more need for prayer.

Our church is old. The building I mean. The sanctuary has a second-story balcony overhanging the sides and the back. This church has been standing for almost 300 years, standing as a beacon of light in a dark world. God has blessed the people of this church in big ways, as they seek to grow in Him and tell others about Him. The student and youth ministry programs are prime examples of God's blessings.

I guess you would call it tradition, but the norm at our church is that the junior high and high school students would sit up in the balcony. It's actually pretty cool. Often times when I am down in front in the sanctuary helping lead worship with the worship band, I will look up into the balcony and see these amazing students. Automatically it brings a smile to my face. I love these students.

Some are singing, some talking, some looking sleepy. I am so thankful that these students are here in church worshipping. Worshipping together with their friends. Hanging out with their friends, in this church setting. Encouraging each other, building each other up. It blesses my heart to see it. I've been known to shed a few tears sometimes, just looking up at these students.

And let us consider how we may spur one another on toward love and good deeds. Let us not give up meeting together, as some are in the habit of doing, but let us encourage one another – and all the more as you see the Day approaching. (Hebrews 10:24-25)

These students are making church and their church friends a priority. So I often revisit that picture in my mind of all those high school students up in the balcony, as I begin to pray for them during lap sixteen. I don't know their individual struggles or challenges or burdens, but God knows. I just lift them up in prayer, and leave the rest to God.

I also pray for the high school seniors who serve as junior high ministry intern leaders. I pray for them to be bold with the Gospel, and yet totally approachable and real. I pray that junior high students will risk it and get to know these seniors, who have so much to offer them. I pray that deep friendships form, bonds of fellowship are built, and God is glorified.

If there's a special student-led Bible study coming up later in the week, or a student mission trip or outreach, I will also pray specifically for that.

BOLD FOR CHRIST

There are so many stories I can share with you about students being bold about sharing the Gospel. These memories often bring tears to my eyes when I think back. One of my favorites occurred during a junior high weekend mission trip to inner city Philadelphia. I was an adult leader of a team of a dozen or so junior high students and some high school senior interns.

We were taking a lunch break in a city park, after a great morning of ministry in the city. There was a gathering of people in the park, about a hundred yards away from us, and music was playing. Hearing the music, one of my junior high students, Chloe, turned to me and said: "Mr Hannig, they're playing our song!" Chloe was right. They were playing one of our favorite worship songs, My Redeemer Lives.

Chloe then said: "Mr Hannig, I think we should go over there." I just love Chloe and her boldness. We were midway through lunch, though, and I wanted our team to have some down time before an equally busy afternoon of ministry. But Chloe persisted. Respectfully, of course. "Mr Hannig, I really think we should go over there."

So we did. I learned something that day. Sometimes you hold onto the rudder, other times, you let it loose. We went over and found another Christian group there, feeding and ministering to a hundred homeless people in the park.

One thing led to the next. Our entire team was now working alongside our new friends, handing out song sheets, Bibles and food, and talking with the homeless people. They had been playing recorded music. We offered to lead worship live, and they welcomed us. So we plugged in our guitars and sang worship songs to the Lord. We even had a couple of our junior high students, on microphone, praying over the people who gathered. Another bold junior high student, Josh, stepped up to the microphone, and preached the Gospel to the crowd, as only a teenager could. What an afternoon!

> *Don't let anyone look down on you because you are young, but set an example for the believers in speech, in life, in faith and in purity. (1 Timothy 4:12)*

These junior high students did just that…

I love the boldness of these students… It's amazing. I pray for that kind of boldness in each of these students.

CHAPTER SEVENTEEN:
Laps 17 & 18

On to lap seventeen. This lap brings more family to mind and to heart. To me, age seventeen means high school upperclassmen and the world beyond. During lap seventeen, I pray for my niece Courtney and my nephew EJ. These two were probably in college when I started doing prayer laps. But seventeen seemed to fit for them at the time, and it reminds me to pray for them now.

Nowadays, both Courtney and EJ are out of college and in the working world. And Courtney is now married to a fine young man. So by virtue of marriage, I include Courtney's husband in my lap seventeen prayer as well. But I was praying for him even before he showed up on the scene.

Initially, my prayers for Courtney and EJ primarily involved their relationship with the Lord, for their future spouses if that's what God's plan called for, for their protection, and for their growth. It is so comforting to know that all things are in God's hands. The more I pray, the more I come to realize, appreciate and embrace that fact.

I'll often expand the scope of my prayers to include their line of work, and the challenges they might be facing in work or in relationships. There are many challenges in being a young adult, including the pressure to try to figure it all out. And the deep desire to do the best they can for themselves and for the ones they love. Plus the world seems to be hardening, becoming a more and more difficult place in which to live as a Christian.

INFLUENCE OF MEDIA

The media seems to be cranking up the volume on negative and sinful messages, telling you who you want to be, how to treat others, and even defining one's body image. There seem to be pressures on all sides to cut corners, or to mistreat others, or to deceive. I pray for them to take the high road in all of life's decisions, the road that would honor God. I pray for them to be tuned in to godly messages, that these messages may direct their steps through daily life. I pray for them to always remain tuned in to God.

It seems the noise coming at us is what you would get from an old school radio. Think circa 1960s. Do you remember the kind? You turned the dial carefully to tune in a particular station, amidst the static. You'd turn the dial to the left, then to the right, until you found the best reception you could get. I also remember liking how it sounded when I spun the tuning dial as fast as I could, with the volume turned up. It made some pretty cool sounds, and a trail of blips, as it caught just an instant of one radio station, then an instant of the next one.

It seems that there is so much noise coming at, well, each of us actually, including you and me. It's up to us to find the station that's broadcasting the Truth. In other words, we search for God's voice. I believe that God's voice is the still small voice (of the awesome and powerful I Am). It takes time, and it takes effort to slowly turn the dial through a lot of garbage stations, until you come to the station with God's still small voice. It's like the gentle whisper that came to Elijah:

> *The Lord said, "Go out and stand on the mountain in the presence of the Lord, for the Lord is about to pass by."*
>
> *Then a great and powerful wind tore the mountains apart and shattered the rocks before the Lord, but the Lord was not in the wind. After the wind there was an earthquake, but the Lord was not in the earthquake. After the earthquake came a fire, but the Lord was not in the fire.*
>
> *And after the fire came a gentle whisper. When Elijah heard it, he pulled his cloak over his face and went out and stood at the mouth of the cave.*

Then a voice said to him, "What are you doing here, Elijah?" (1 Kings 19:11-13)

God showed up to Elijah as the gentle whisper. The all-powerful One came as a soft whisper. Amazing. Similarly, we need to look past the noises that would attract our attention, and seek the voice of the One who calls us.

One more thing about the world's noise, as it seeks our complete attention. It seeks to distract us from the One to whom we ought to be paying attention. We need to turn away from the sinful noise. But what do we turn towards?

Finally, brothers, whatever is true, whatever is noble, whatever is right, whatever is pure, whatever is lovely, whatever is admirable – if anything is excellent or praiseworthy – think about such things. (Philippians 4:8)

There is plenty of godly music, godly arts, godly people around for us to enjoy and grow with. God will always balance His "dos" and His "don'ts" for us. We need to pray for one another to develop His eyes in us, so that we may see things as He does.

TWENTY-SOMETHINGS

Similarly, lap eighteen brings to mind a number of now twenty-something men and women of God, who I've come to know through student ministry or mission work at my church. With many of them I've had the pleasure of working shoulder-to-shoulder in junior high or high school ministry. In that sense, they are brothers and sisters, and co-laborers. My mental short list of lap eighteen people includes about a dozen godly men and women, and now there are some of their spouses added as well.

One thing I've really enjoyed and felt led to do is what I call the "ministry of meals." Basically, it's getting together with one or more young adults over a meal, or a cup of coffee. There's something about gathering over a meal which opens the door to conversation, shares love and welcomes God's presence.

Lately, I've really enjoyed gathering a small group of seminary students and spouses, who each help with our church student ministry. We simply gather for a meal, my treat. It may be the best spent part of my tithe. We let the Spirit have His way. And we just have fun being together. And among the messages I try to convey to these brothers and sisters are that I love each of them, that I really enjoy working with them, and that I'm proud of them.

I pray for these young men and women of God. I see many of the same challenges for Courtney and EJ as for these men and women. The world keeps hammering them. Maybe it was no different in early Biblical times. But it just seems to be more amplified, and more steady these days. Being a Christian is truly swimming upstream. It is all the more reason to pray for strength of will, and a heart for God. It is not a time for the weak of heart. Rather, the contrary:

For God did not give us a spirit of timidity, but a spirit of power, of love and of self-discipline. (2 Timothy 1:7)

So, yes, I pray for their individual relationships with the Lord, for their future spouses, for their protection, and for their growth. But beyond that, I pray for their boldness in following the Lord. I pray for their love for Him and for others to grow. And I pray for their self-discipline to grow.

CHRISTIAN DISCIPLINE

Discipline is not a popular thing these days. At first, the word just sounds like a burden. But with the Lord, discipline is a key to growth in Him. And these days, it's a must-have. And Jesus promises that His yoke is not a burden.

"Come to me, all you who are weary and burdened, and I will give you rest. Take my yoke upon you and learn from me, for I am gentle and humble in heart, and you will find rest for your souls. For my yoke is easy and my burden is light." (Matthew 11:28-30)

CHAPTER EIGHTEEN:
Laps 19 & 20

On to laps nineteen, and then twenty. What would these numbers mean to you? Here's a hint for what they symbolize for me:

> *Give thanks to the Lord, for he is good; his love endures forever. (1 Chronicles 16:34)*

And another:

> *Be joyful always; pray continually; give thanks in all circumstances, for this is God's will for you in Christ Jesus. (1 Thessalonians 5:16-18)*

Laps nineteen and twenty end a set of twenty laps in a spirit of thankfulness. And one way I like to end my prayer time is to simply say to God: thank You and I love You.

So, when I swim lap nineteen, I am simply

reflecting on all God has done, and giving Him thanks. I really cannot rush through any of that. It causes me to go deep, to pause and reflect once more on the past few hours. Or perhaps to reflect on what's happened so far this day. Sometimes I'll look back on the entire week.

It's easy to blow through the events of a day, maybe just focusing on the highlights, the memorable events. Among them are the moments when it seems easier to see God's hand at work. But I realize that God is always at work in and around me. And I realize that even when I'm doing my best to look for God's hand at work, I might see one thing while missing a thousand others.

MEDITATE

So I try to stop and really meditate on all of the little things I can see that God has done. The gifts He's given, which I so often take for granted. The lives He's touched. The relationship with a family member or a friend which He has graced. Simply thanking Him for the simple gift of life, or even the next breath.

When I really slow down and reflect, I realize that His works are everywhere. And I am overwhelmed with thanks for all that God has done. At the same time, I realize I deserve none of it. Yet He provides.

I also pray that the things God has done will take root, and will grow. As you'll see, this prayer is a natural transition into lap twenty. For example, if it appears that God has gotten a friend's attention, I pray that he or she is eager to begin or continue a relationship with the Lord, and that that relationship will grow. So lap nineteen is mainly a backward-looking and reflective prayer time of thanks.

THANKS IN ADVANCE

Lap twenty, on the other hand, is a forward-looking prayer time of thanks. During lap twenty, I am eagerly anticipating all that God will do, and thanking Him in advance for all of that. God is so powerful and so loving. I sometimes imagine myself as a small child cuddled in the palm of God's huge hand. I am warmly embraced and protected by Him. He is the God of the past, the present and the future.

Here are some examples of the things I pray in my forward-looking prayer of thanks. I may meditate on a student ministry event coming up, like a retreat or mission trip, and thank God in advance for having His way with students and leaders there. I may think about an upcoming event in a family or friend's life, and thank God for being present in their life and in that event.

I may thank God for His hand in upcoming work events, for example, for relationships to be built during an upcoming business trip. Or perhaps for His guidance on when I should consider retirement and what might come next. I can also simply open my heart and mind and thank God for whatever is ahead.

Think, for a moment, about the concept of anticipating what God will do and thanking Him for that, even before it happens. And trying to do that without any preconceived notions about what God will do in the future. I think that's easier said than done.

Even as I sit and write this chapter, I see that when I'm thanking God in advance, what comes to mind most readily are positive things I'm hoping for Him to make happen. I think it's easy to thank Him in advance for the healing of relationships, the healing of disease. We can easily imagine God blessing us and those we love with success, with peace, with happiness. And He does provide good things.

Sometimes, though, I think God gives or permits things which do not appear on the surface to be blessings. Instead, they appear to be harmful or bad. For example, consider an illness, or a loss. Or an accident, or pain. Those things are hard to accept. And it's sometimes hard to see God's hand in an apparent loss or in pain.

Scripture reassures us, though, that God can and does use *all* things for His good.

> *And we know that in all things God works for the good of those who love him, who have been called according to his purpose. (Romans 8:28)*

At times like these, when it's hard to see God's good in what happens, I think about the Scripture reference to God, providing as a Father:

> *"Which of you fathers, if your son asks for a*

118

fish, will give him a snake instead? Or if he asks for an egg, will give him a scorpion? If you then, though you are evil, know how to give good gifts to your children, how much more will your Father in heaven give the Holy Spirit to those who ask him!" (Luke 11:11-13)

Scripture calls us to give ourselves totally to God. We are to trust Him as the loving Father that He is.

Trust in the Lord with all your heart and lean not on your own understanding. (Proverbs 3:5)

The more we trust God, the more we will be able to really thank Him in advance for what He will do. He truly knows what is best for us, and He provides for us. So, as I try to thank God in advance for what He will do, it becomes so clear to me that I need to trust Him more. In my heart I need to release my family and friends into God's loving hands, knowing He's got it covered. I need to stop worrying about people and events, and about the future. When I worry, I allow my anxieties about tomorrow to consume this amazing gift of today.

Therefore do not worry about tomorrow, for tomorrow will worry about itself. Each day has enough trouble of its own. (Matthew 6:34)

Instead, I need to look to Him. I need to seek Him with even greater desire.

> *But seek first his kingdom and his righteousness, and all these things will be given you as well. (Matthew 6:33)*

I realize it's really a thankfulness woven in faith that I'm trying to express. Deep down, I know He knows best.

So laps nineteen and twenty are thankful laps. Thank You, Lord, for what You've done. And thank You, Lord, for what You will do. If our hearts are truly thankful, we are humbled. That is a great position to be in, and it allows God to further work within us.

After lap twenty, I may be done swimming for the day. In that case, what better way to end my prayer laps time than to tell God: thank You. Period. However, if I'm ready to continue on to the next set of twenty laps, I end this first set saying thank you to God. I then continue on to lap one again, focusing my prayer once again on God: Father, Son and Holy Spirit. And so, the cycle continues.

CHAPTER NINETEEN:
Strength & Motivation

While this book describes the way that I currently do my prayer laps, I imagine that some things will change over time. For example, prayer laps could take on different or additional meaning, and my prayer focus for a particular lap could change. I need to be open to that, and not get stuck in a mechanical routine. Moreover, my prayer time needs to constantly renew itself. I should be constantly asking the question: God, what would You have me do? And then go there.

Now, to be candid, doing prayer laps requires both strength and motivation. Strength of body. Strength of soul. Strength of will. And it requires a motivation that gets me out of my comfort zone and pushing my body. And out of the warm house and into the cold swimming pool.

STRENGTH

Let's first talk about strength. Here is a story, from many years ago, which is still near and dear to my heart. I have been working for a large corporation for over thirty years. It has been one of many gifts bestowed from God. I am so grateful for the many friends at work who have been a blessing to me, whether they know it or not, over the years. I can especially remember, shortly after my wife Nancy died, when I was working in an oil refinery, where I had a pretty significant assignment.

It was almost like a perfect storm: single dad, just getting over losing his wife, young son two or three years old and growing fast, and heavy responsibilities at work.

There was an oil spill near the refinery, in a large, navigable waterway. The company had asked me to take on the responsibility of representing them in legal settings (I'm an engineer, remember) and to work with a team of lawyers. These were pretty high stakes, and it was all new to me and pretty intimidating. I accepted, and began working with new colleagues, including several lawyers. But there was one attorney who I drew close to. I found out that he was a Christian, too. His name was Dave.

Dave would receive subpoenas sent by government agencies, which would require the company to search its files and produce documents that were related in some way to the oil spill. My new role was to be responsible for representing the document search and review action to the courts.

I can remember one subpoena in particular. Dave faxed a copy of it to me, along with a cover letter. On the cover letter, he wrote something like: "John, here's another subpoena..." But what I remember clearly was how he ended his note: "...Philippians 4:13."

Now, at this time, I didn't know that Scripture verse. I had not really gotten into reading my Bible as yet. Now it's one of my life verses, you might say. So I reached into my briefcase and pulled out my Bible, and looked up this verse. Here's what it says:

I can do everything through him who gives me strength. (Philippians 4:13)

Dave was acknowledging this incoming request would require a lot of work, for sure. But he was also reminding me that there is One who is far greater. Greater than all else. Jesus conquered death, and He did it for you, and for me. I can indeed do all things through Jesus Christ, who strengthens me. Thanks, Dave, for the encouragement.

MOTIVATION

So I can do all things, through Christ. He gives me the strength. But just because I *can* do it, doesn't mean I *will* do it. What about motivation? There are times when I really don't feel like praying. I'm not proud of that at all, nor do I like it when I feel like that. But I'm being honest. When I look back at a time like that, I often discover that it's a time when

I've been dabbling with temptation and falling to sin. Sin has kept me from praying. And praying is the very thing I need.

At times like these, it is good to have an additional and separate motivator encouraging you to pray. The need for physical exercise has often been that separate motivator for me. It's often gotten me into the pool and swimming, and that's gotten me into praying again. I didn't feel like praying, but I felt the need to exercise, and as a result, I'm doing both.

Conversely, there are also times when I just really don't feel like exercising. Maybe I'm physically or emotionally tired. Maybe I'm down and just don't feel like doing much of anything. At times like these, again, it is a good thing to have a separate motivator, leading you in the same direction. My need for prayer has often gotten me into the pool and swimming. I didn't feel like exercising, but I felt the need to pray, and as a result, I'm doing both.

HUMBLED & MOTIVATED

A few years ago, I went on a company-sponsored course which taught me some important things about motivation. It was a course designed to get each employee to improve their overall health. Not just their physical health, but especially that. The way they tried to get each employee motivated was very smart.

They first let you pick a training machine, such as a treadmill or a stationary bike, to use for your workout. Then they had you steadily increase your speed and push your heart rate well beyond your comfort zone. They wanted you to push your body to a point where you were no longer able to talk. It was a very humbling experience for each of us. I had thought I was in pretty good shape, but I found there was so much more room for improvement.

Then they had you sit in an egg-shaped device, which measures body fat. They said it was like the one they use at NASA, therefore capable of great accuracy. Again, I was expecting some pretty good results, since I had been working out. For men, they said 20% or less was good. So I was expecting something in the high teens.

When they gave out individual body fat results, in an envelope for privacy, to each person in the room, the room went quiet. You could hear a pin drop. My result came in at 22.6%, a far cry from the high teens I had expected. Humbling. Judging from the silence in the room, most of my colleagues were also surprised with their higher than expected results.

All that, plus blood test results served as ample motivators for me and the others in the class. We all worked hard from that point forward. And I think we all got a lot out of the course as a result. Unless there's a perceived need, there's no motivation. I realize that I need to pray regularly and exercise regularly. And I need to be growing and caring for my spiritual and physical health.

I will say that over the years I have found there is a strong benefit in linking spiritual exercise with physical exercise. There's a synergistic effect when my prayer and exercise "buckets" are filled. There's a feeling of accomplishment, satisfaction and completeness. There's a sense of wholeness and health within me. Plus, I feel more alive. It's worth it.

CHAPTER TWENTY:
Your Turn

Hopefully, you have come away with an understanding of the prayer laps concept of merging spiritual and physical workouts. Again, this concept does not belong to me. It came from the Lord, and I gladly share it with you in the hopes that it blesses you. How you might use the prayer laps idea is, of course, totally up to you.

Here are a few things you may want to consider in applying the prayer laps concept to your life. What time of day is typically best for you to work out? Some prefer early in the day, others the afternoon or evening. I am a morning person, so my preference is to do my workouts early in the day. I think of prayer as more of a continual conversation throughout the day. As a result, deciding when to do my prayer laps is more driven by the workout timing that works best for me. In any event, choose the time of day best for you, one with the greatest chance of continued success.

Another consideration is location. Where would you be doing your prayer laps? You may have membership to a gym or a pool, and plan to work out there. But that's not a requirement. You may want to do your workout at home, or outside, or in and around your neighborhood.

With what type of workout would you consider using the prayer laps idea? You might be a runner. Or a walker. If you run on a treadmill, you might change your prayer focus every minute or two, or every quarter mile or half mile. If you run outside or through your neighborhood, you might assign a specific prayer focus for each block, or group of blocks. If you run at a track, you might change your prayer focus every lap of a quarter mile track.

You might be doing resistance training. You might be doing sit-ups or push-ups. You might be doing many reps on a specific piece of equipment. In that case, you might change your prayer focus after every set of reps. Or you might change after a specific exercise is completed. Or when you finish working out at a piece of equipment.

You might also consider using the prayer laps idea while stretching. You could change your prayer focus after each stretching routine. Or after stretching a specific muscle group.

And so, now it's your turn.

I don't know where you are in your walk with the Lord. I don't know what your prayer life is like. And you might not even like to exercise. But, I encourage you to be thoughtful and creative with this concept of prayer laps.

Think of who or what you might pray about. Choose a physical workout or exercise that will work for you. Then develop a plan, including time of day, how many days per week and location. Without a plan, nothing is likely to happen.

If you think about it, once you make it a priority to either exercise or to pray, the rest is easy. Let's say you've decided to exercise for a half hour. If you decide to combine prayer and exercise for that half hour, the prayer time is, in a sense, free. It doesn't require any additional time and both exercise and prayer have been completed.

YOU CAN DO IT

You probably know the feeling, how great you feel once you've completed a hard physical workout. And it's an even greater feeling when both your prayer and exercise workouts are done. You feel like both "buckets" are filled once again.

> *Have nothing to do with godless myths and old wives' tales; rather, train yourself to be godly. For physical training is of some value, but godliness has value for all things, holding promise for both the present life and the life to come. (1 Timothy 4:7-8)*

Physical training is good, but spiritual training is better. If you can do both at the same time, even better.

One final thought regarding putting prayer laps into practice. It will take motivation, yes. But it will also require that you give it priority in your life, and in your busy day-to-day schedule. I think it's the kind of thing that may be difficult to start. But once you've begun, and have felt the early benefits of doing it, I think you'll find it easier to maintain. So start small. Take small steps. See how that goes, and take it from there.

Give it a try for a week. Like the sneaker commercial, "Just Do It." If it works for you, give glory to God. And keep doing it. Enjoy your rejuvenated and enlivened prayer time, and enjoy feeling better physically.

> *Therefore, if anyone is in Christ, he is a new creation; the old has gone, the new has come! (2 Corinthians 5:17)*

It might just change your world. It could also change the world around you.

EPILOGUE

So there it is. Prayer laps. Looking back on the preceding chapters, I see that there are stories of my life woven in and out of many chapters. My life has been far better than I deserve. God has blessed me richly. I hope that comes through, along with my gratefulness to Him.

During the writing of Prayer Laps, I decided to start training for a full marathon. 26.2 miles. You might think that's a bit crazy for me at 50-plus. And you're right. Why would I do that? I had enjoyed running each of the two half marathons, and I ran them with family. It was gratifying to work hard and prepare for each run, and then to cross the finish line, to accomplish the goal. Plus, I had now gotten used to the more or less daily discipline of running.

I thought about what I would think when, say, I'm 75 years old, looking back on life. I know I've been blessed with an amazing life so far. I figured that I didn't want to get to the finish line of life just doing half of something. While the half marathons were great accomplishments, for sure, part of me was thinking that a half marathon seemed a little like half a home run. I decided I did not want to finish my life having completed only two half home runs. I wanted a whole home run. So it was decided. I'd run a marathon. One marathon. One and done.

TRAINING

I googled "marathon training schedule" and found several training plans to follow. I chose one for beginners, which seemed appropriate. Since this was a one time goal, I looked for a marathon which would be flat in elevation and for which the temperature would be perfect for me. And I got to work...

Each week I would track my daily and weekly mileage and then compare it to my training plan. Early in the training, I had gotten to a point at which I needed to push my long run for the week up to 10 miles. So I decided to give prayer laps a shot on the local high school quarter mile track.

Up until that point, I had only used the prayer laps concept for swimming. From the beginning of this book, I have suggested that the prayer laps concept works for swimming, running and other workouts as well. Here was a chance for me to see if that was indeed true.

A while back, after watching a local high school football game, I left the field by walking across the running track which surrounded the football field. As I did, I was immediately reminded how comfortable and cushioned the track was, compared to the unforgiving road pavement I normally run on.

Cushioned seemed much better.

So I started my run through a nearby neighborhood, and then headed to this local high school track. I took a 4 mile run to get to the track. From there I ran twenty laps on the quarter mile track. As I ran each lap, I meditated on the same prayer laps pattern I had used for the pool.

So how did it go? I found the run to be refreshing, and a lot easier than I had expected, in part due to the prayer time, in part due to the soft track. I also found that, since it takes me longer to run a quarter mile than it does to swim one lap, my time in prayer for each lap was longer. That was refreshing too, as it gave me time to explore and expand the areas I'd pray about.

That day I ran 10 miles and did prayer laps at the running track. It works....

> *Therefore, since we are surrounded by such a great cloud of witnesses, let us throw off everything that hinders and the sin that so easily entangles, and let us run with perseverance the race marked out for us. Let us fix our eyes on Jesus, the author and perfecter of our faith, who for the joy set before him endured the cross, scorning its shame, and sat down at the right hand of the throne of God. (Hebrews 12:1-2)*

I continued using the prayer laps concept at the running track, even as the long run mileage goals grew to 15 miles, then to 20 miles. It continued to work. And to bless.

My body was taking more of a pounding, though, with the more intense training. One thing I really began learning was how important a Sabbath was for my training. And for my life.

So I ran hard six days a week. And on Sunday, I took a Sabbath from training. No running that day. Instead, I walked to church – maybe I should do that more often… And I'm also learning to make that day a Sabbath for not just body, but for soul as well.

Remember the Sabbath day by keeping it holy. (Exodus 20:8)

Life is about balance.

RACE DAY

Race day came at the Jersey Shore, April 2014. The weather was perfect. The locals were out to support and cheer on several thousand runners. The atmosphere was fun and encouraging. Though I didn't know anyone else who was running that day, I made plenty of friends along the run. My goal was to finish the marathon. Period. No time goals, just to finish.

Towards the end of the run, with five miles to go, I knew I would finish, but I was starting to slow down a bit. It was just then that a friend of mine from work, Ken, called out to me from the sidewalk. He had come down to the race to encourage me on. He told me he was going to run with me the final few miles. What an amazing friend! So we ran... And talked...

A mile or two later, another friend from church, Steve, was riding his bicycle. He too had come to encourage me and to ride along with me... Thank You, Lord, for the great gift of friends...

A friend loves at all times, and a brother is born for adversity. (Proverbs 17:17)

I needed encouragement, from friends. And God provided just that, through Ken and Steve.

I crossed the finish line... What a feeling... And what a journey... Thank You, Lord...

I wonder what's next...

ABOUT THE AUTHOR

John would describe himself, first, as a sinner saved by grace. He is a widower, a father and now a grandfather. He has completed a successful career as an engineer in the petroleum industry, but his heart and his passion are, and have long been, in student ministry. He finds working with students both challenging and uplifting – he'd say it keeps him young. He is a church elder, a Sunday school teacher, and worship leader. He treasures the gift of time with family and friends. He loves students, music, the outdoors, sports, cookouts, being active, and, oh yes, writing.